The
Key
Comprehension
Routine Grades 4-12

Joan Sedita

Keys to Literacy®

319 Newburyport Tpke, Suite 205
Rowley, MA 01969
978-948-8511 www.keystoliteracy.com

Cover Design and Text Layout: Peggy MacNeil

ISBN 0-9786106-0-1

Printed in the United States of America

Published and Distributed by

Keys to Literacy®

319 Newburyport Tpke, Suite 205
Rowley, MA 01969
978-948-8511 **www.keystoliteracy.com**

Dedication

To my husband Joe and my children Jay and Marco –
they are the keys to my happiness.

Acknowledgements

The first edition of this book, published in 2003, was titled The Key Three Routine. It was the result of my years of work with students and teachers beginning in 1975. Their desire to learn and teach comprehension was the motivation for that first edition, and it was used as the basis for professional development that was delivered to thousands of teachers throughout the country. For this second edition, I have changed the title to *The Key Comprehension Routine* and made changes based on feedback from training sessions and to reflect more recent research findings regarding effective comprehension instruction.

I would like to thank all of the teachers who participated in the professional development that inspired this second edition. I am also grateful to the talented Keys to Literacy trainers who deliver the professional development and follow-up support to teachers so they can successfully implement the program. Their experience and insight contributed significantly to this book. In particular, I would like to thank Becky DeSmith, Shauna Cotte, Noel Foy, and Kathe Simons for their overall contributions to the book, and to Becky specifically for her contribution to the question generation chapter. Final thanks go to my Keys to Literacy partner, Brad Neuenhaus, for helping our company grow to serve more teachers and students.

TABLE OF CONTENTS

PART IV: Putting It All Together

Chapter 5: Combining Activities

Chapter 6: Implementing The Routine Across a School

Introduction

The Key Comprehension Routine is a combination of comprehension, writing and study strategies that helps students understand and learn content information. The routine helps teachers provide effective comprehension instruction using existing subject-area material.

This book is organized into four parts:

✳ **Part I: Overview of Comprehension Instruction**

> Chapter 1 provides an overview of *The Key Comprehension Routine* and why content teachers benefit from using a strategy routine. The chapter reviews instructional practices including explicit instruction, gradual release of responsibility, scaffolding, and differentiated instruction. Chapter 2 presents a review of the research about effective comprehension instruction.

✳ **Part II: Essential Comprehension Skills**

> Chapter 3 presents suggestions, techniques, and practice activities for teaching main idea skills. The chapter offers a sequence for teaching main ideas, from simple categorizing to paragraph-level main ideas – as well as finding main ideas in lengthy reading selections. Chapter 4 presents suggestions for the use of think alouds and text discussion to teach comprehension skills. Chapter 4 reviews how text structure at the sentence, paragraph, and full-text levels affects comprehension.

✳ **Part III: The Four Activities in *The Key Comprehension Routine***

> Here you will find a section for each of the Routine's four activities: Top-Down Topic Webs, Two-Column Notes, Summary, and Question Generation. In addition to an explanation of each activity, these sections provide suggestions for the direct instruction of each strategy.

✳ **Part IV: Putting It All Together**

> Chapter 5 provides suggestions for combining the four activities, as well as applying them to different content-specific material. Chapter 6 offers recommendations for school-wide implementation of *The Key Comprehension Routine*.

Finally, we have provided reproducible templates discussed throughout the book, classroom examples of *The Key Comprehension Routine* activities, and references.

The Key Comprehension Routine is based on the author's work beginning in 1975 with thousands of students and teachers in schools throughout the country. The author developed main idea, note taking, and summarizing instruction methods and materials during the 1970's and 1980's when she was working with struggling learners at the Landmark School in Massachusetts. During the 1990's and the first years of the new millennium, she worked with a number of public middle schools and high schools to develop a model for school-wide integration of comprehension strategy instruction in all content classes. The model, formerly named the Key Three Routine, is currently being used in classrooms throughout the United States.

Who Should Use This Book?

This book is for educators who work with students in grades 4 – 12. Content classroom teachers will learn a systematic, easy-to-use model for incorporating comprehension strategy instruction using their existing content material, class work, and assignments. Specialists, such as reading teachers, special education teachers, Title I teachers, and reading paraprofessionals will learn a comprehension instruction model that they can support in inclusive classrooms and reinforce through supplemental instruction. Administrators will learn a flexible model for comprehension instruction that can be incorporated in individual classrooms, by grade-level or teams of teachers, and on a school-wide basis. Parents will also find *The Key Comprehension Routine* helpful as they assist their children with reading, homework, and test study.

Part I

Overview of Comprehension Instruction

Chapter 1

What is *The Key Comprehension Routine?*

The Key Comprehension Routine teaches students in grades 4-12 a combination of comprehension, writing, and study strategies to comprehend and learn content information from reading, lecture, and classroom discussion. The routine emphasizes the integration of comprehension strategy instruction with existing content teaching materials. *The Key Comprehension Routine* can be used in any subject area (e.g., science, social studies, English-language arts, math). An adapted version of for grades K-3 is also available. All students benefit from *The Key Comprehension Routine*, and it is particularly helpful for struggling readers.

The Key Comprehension Routine includes main idea skills, text structure, and four strategy activities: top-down topic webs, two-column notes, summary, and question generation. Figure A depicts the Routine's components.

Figure A

Components	Specifics
Main Idea Skills and Text Structure	<ul><li>Identifying and stating main ideas</li><li>Categorizing</li><li>Paragraph level main ideas</li><li>Text structure</li></ul>
Activity 1: Top-Down Topic Webs	<ul><li>Based on reading</li><li>Based on instructional topic</li><li>Before writing</li></ul>
Activity 2: Two-Column Notes	<ul><li>Detailed notes</li><li>Big-picture notes</li></ul>
Activity 3: Summary	<ul><li>Limited summary</li><li>Big-picture summary</li></ul>
Activity 4: Question Generation	<ul><li>Using main ideas from text headings, topic webs, notes</li><li>Levels of questions using Bloom's Taxonomy</li></ul>

The four activities in *The Key Comprehension Routine* can be used before, during, and after reading or classroom lessons. They can be applied to a single reading passage (e.g., newspaper article), a lengthy reading selection (e.g., textbook chapter, short story), a classroom lecture or lesson, or an entire unit of study taught over several weeks. In short, *The Key Comprehension Routine* activities help students *reconfigure* content to make it more accessible and engage students to become more active learners. There is an old proverb that says, "When I hear it I forget, when I see it I remember, and when I do it I understand." Generating top-down topic webs, two-column notes, questions and summaries represent the proverb's last element, "doing it," the strongest contributor to improved comprehension.

The Key Comprehension Routine combines a set of activities identified by research as the most effective for improving comprehension (see Chapter 2, *Comprehension Instruction*). The activities can be used individually or combined (see Chapter 5, *Combining Activities*). Although *The Key Comprehension Routine* can be used by an individual teacher, it is best used by a team of teachers or as a school-wide program (see Chapter 6, *Implementing the Routine Across a School*). For schools that are implementing a Response to Intervention (RtI) model, the routine is considered Tier I instruction when used in content classrooms (i.e., research-based literacy instruction for all students) and Tier II instruction when additional support and guided practice are provided by intervention specialists (i.e., supplemental, individualized instruction for struggling students).

Why Do Content Teachers Need a Routine?

A significant body of research identifies the most effective practices for teaching comprehension, but much of this research has not found its way into content classrooms. Many content teachers assume that their students have already learned comprehension strategies, or teachers may rely on textbook publishers to provide comprehension aids such as end-of-chapter questions, study guides, or graphic organizers. However, research has found that content teachers are in an excellent position to teach students how to use comprehension strategies (Kamil et al., 2008). The most compelling reason to implement a program like *The Key Comprehension Routine* is to ensure that teachers incorporate comprehension instruction that is research-based.

A Consistent Set of Strategies

A second reason to use *The Key Comprehension Routine* is to provide a consistent set of comprehension strategy activities as students move from grade to grade and class to class. To be sure, there are numerous books and courses for teachers about how to teach comprehension strategies; a quick search of the internet yields hundreds of graphic organizers and dozens of strategy activities. With so many options, teachers can easily become overwhelmed by the choices and – even worse – students become confused when they must learn different formats and strategies for multiple teachers. *The Key Comprehension Routine* offers a basic set of fundamental strategies that can be consistently implemented across subject areas. Students who are exposed to a strategy routine over several grades benefit from repeated, long-term exposure and practice with a small set of strategy activities, enabling students to use them independently.

Many teachers already incorporate strategy activities into their classroom instruction. When teachers implement *The Key Comprehension Routine*, they do not stop using other strategy activities (e.g., outlining, other types of graphic organizers, different question generation models); rather, the idea is for students to see the same small set of foundational activities in all their classes. When students see a basic set of strategies applied in all subjects, the repetition enables them to more readily learn the strategies.

Activity 1: Assessing Current Use of Comprehension Strategies

Directions: Make a list of all the comprehension strategies you use with students. Place the strategies in the appropriate column below. Circle one or two of the strategies that work best with your students.		
Before Reading	**During Reading**	**After Reading**

How is *The Key Comprehension Routine* Taught?

There are several instructional practices that enable teachers to meet a wide variety of learning styles and needs when they are teaching comprehension strategies. Collectively, these principles are the hallmark of differentiated instruction. Teachers should provide explicit and direct instruction of comprehension strategies. Significant modeling, guided practice, small-group collaboration, and opportunities to practice application of comprehension strategies in different subjects are critical. Each of these principles is described in further detail below.

Explicit and Direct Instruction Through Modeling

The National Reading Panel (2000) found that while some readers acquire strategies informally, explicit strategy instruction is highly effective in enhancing comprehension. For students with learning problems, the RAND study (Snow, 2002) found that successful instruction is characterized by explicit modeling by the teacher, additional opportunities for practice with feedback, skillful adjustments to the learner's level, and the reader's mindful engagement with the purpose for reading. In her synthesis of the research on adolescent literacy, Curtis (2002) writes:

> Higher order strategic processing is responsive to instruction, particularly when the instruction is long-term, includes modeling of the strategy, provides frequent and informed practice of the strategy used, and emphasizes when and where the strategy can be used ... information that seems to be best gained when teachers and students model the process and talk about its use. (p.6)

Explicit instruction of comprehension strategies leads to improvement in text understanding and information use. The National Reading Panel states:

> Instruction in comprehension strategies is carried out by a classroom teacher who demonstrates, models, or guides the reader on their acquisition and use. When these procedures have been acquired, the reader becomes independent of the teacher. Using them, the reader can effectively interact with the text without assistance. Readers who are not explicitly taught these procedures are unlikely to learn, develop, or use them spontaneously. (p. 4-40)

The Key Comprehension Routine promotes explicit strategy instruction embedded in the context of specific academic areas.

Gradual Release of Responsibility

The Gradual Release of Responsibility Model (Pearson & Gallagher, 1983) is an effective approach for teaching comprehension strategies. This can be described as an *I do it, we do it, you do it* model of instruction (see Figure B).

In this approach to teaching, the teacher presents a strategy to the class and models its use, including by "thinking out loud" (*I do it*). The teacher then has the students practice applying the strategy as a whole group or in small groups (*we do it*). This practice should be guided by the teacher, who provides feedback. Eventually, students can apply the strategy independently (*you do it*). Students require different amounts of practice in order to reach independence, and some may need additional instruction outside the classroom for extra practice.

Figure B

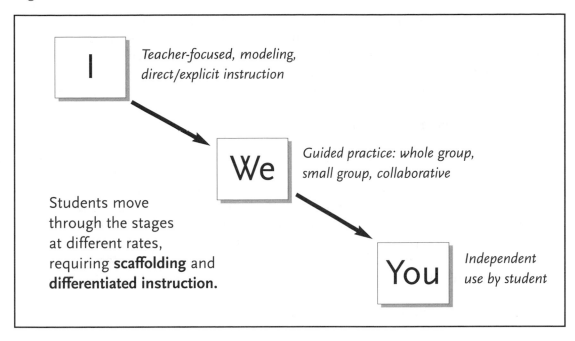

Scaffolding and Differentiated Instruction

The term *scaffold* refers to "teacher support of a learner through dialogue, questioning, conversation, and non-verbal modeling, in which the learner attempts literacy tasks that could not be done without assistance" (Peterson et al., 2000, pp. 17-18). Scaffolding centers on the notion of providing readers with support as they learn to read. Research indicates that scaffolding must take place across the curriculum and that reading strategies that are not supported by content teachers are much less likely to be acquired, especially by struggling secondary readers (Gaskins, 1998).

Dickson, Simmons, and Kame'enui (1995) suggest four types of scaffolding:

* **Teacher/peer scaffolding.** Occurs across the continuum, with more support occurring when new concepts, tasks, or strategies are introduced. Support is gradually decreased as students gain proficiency and assume more responsibility.

* **Content scaffolding.** The teacher first introduces simpler concepts and skills and then slowly guides students through more challenging concepts and skills.

* **Task scaffolding.** The student proceeds from easier to more difficult tasks and activities.

* **Material scaffolding.** A variety of materials are used to guide students' thinking, including partially completed graphic organizers or templates.

Differentiated instruction demands that a teacher proactively plan varied approaches to what students need to learn, how they will learn it, and how they can express what they have learned in order to learn as much and as efficiently as possible (Tomlinson, 2003). Differentiation also entails designing instruction to suit individual student needs rather than using a standardized approach to instruction that assumes all students learn the same way.

Mastery Through Repetition and Review

When students learn information or a strategy at an automatic level, they have learned it so thoroughly that they can use it with little or no conscious attention (Sedita, 1989). Information must be at an automatic level, or mastery level, to be used as a foundation to learn something new. Practice is the key to becoming automatic, and newer or more novel information requires more repeated exposure and practice to become automatic.

Using Collaboration to Practice Strategies

Practicing the application of comprehension strategies cooperatively in pairs or small groups promotes reading comprehension (National Reading Panel, 2000; Klingner et al., 2001). When teachers provide the cognitive structure and instruct students to interact over the use of reading comprehension strategies, this leads to an increase in the learning of the strategies, promotes intellectual discussion, and increases reading comprehension. *The Key Comprehension Routine* incorporates the use of small collaborative groups to practice learning and using main idea skills, top-down topic webs, two-column notes, summarizing, and question generation.

Alignment to the Common Core State Standards

As of 2011, almost all states had adopted the Common Core State Standards (CCSS, 2010). The K-12 literacy standards are organized into four broad categories:

* Reading Standards
* Writing Standards
* Speaking and Listening Standards
* Language Standards

The Key Comprehension Routine is closely aligned with the Literature and Informational Text, Writing, and Speaking and Listening standards for grades K-12.
The routine's alignment to specific standards is detailed in Figure C. In general, Keys to Literacy programs are aligned with the following goals and research base of the CCSS:

* The reading standards for literature and informational text place significant emphasis on careful analytic reading of different types of increasingly complex text. *The Key Comprehension Routine* teaches strategies for analytic reading as well as routines for applying these strategies consistently across grades and subjects. These strategies include identifying main ideas, generating and answering questions at all levels of Bloom's Taxonomy, summarizing, and taking

* The reading standards call for greater exposure to and instruction for reading informational text starting in the early grades.

* A major goal of the reading and writing standards is for students to use comprehension strategies independently. The standards specifically list main idea/detail skills and summarizing, both major components of *The Key Comprehension Routine.*

* The writing standards emphasize the ability to write arguments and informative text based on relevant and sufficient evidence, including the application of

organizing strategies. *The Key Comprehension Routine* teaches students to identify main ideas and relevant details while reading meta-cognitively. Through the use of Top-Down Topic Webs and Two-Column Notes, it also teaches students to organize text evidence.

✳ Both the reading and writing standards specifically address language structures at the sentence, paragraph, and discourse levels. *The Key Comprehension Routine* addresses sentence, paragraph, and broader narrative and informational text structures in all subject areas.

✳ The speaking and listening standards emphasize student collaboration with peers to converse and share ideas. A significant component of *The Key Comprehension Routine* is the use of small-group collaboration to practice comprehension strategies.

✳ The writing and speaking and listening standards address the importance of teaching students how to organize ideas before writing and presenting information orally. *The Key Comprehension Routine* teaches the use of Top-Down Topic Webs, Two-Column Notes, and a Summary Template to organize ideas and information before writing or speaking.

✳ All of the reading and writing standards stress that students should read and write regularly. *The Key Comprehension Routine* emphasizes explicit instruction in foundational reading and writing skills with significant guided practice until students reach the stage of independent use.

Figure C

Alignment to the Common Core State Standards

Category	Specific Standard
Reading Standards – Literature & Informational Text: K-5 & 6-12	• Key Ideas & Details: #1, #2 • Craft & Structure: #4, #5 • Range of Reading & Level of Text Complexity: #10
Reading Standards for Literacy in History/Social Studies, Science, & Technical Subjects: 6-12	• Key Ideas & Details: #1, #2 • Craft & Structure: #4, #5 • Integration of Knowledge & Ideas: #8 • Range of Reading & Level of Text Complexity: #10
Writing Standards for Literacy in History/Social Studies, Science & Technical Subjects: 6-12	• Text Types & Purposes: #1, #2 • Research to Build & Present Knowledge: #7, #8, #9 • Range of Writing: #10
Speaking & Listening Standards: K-5 & 6-12	• Comprehension & Collaboration: #1 • Presentation of Knowledge & Ideas: #4

Professional Development for *The Key Comprehension Routine*

Professional development must be efficient and relate directly to what teachers are doing in their classrooms. Teachers need a basic routine that can be applied easily to any reading and content material. Given the limited budgets facing most schools today, it is also essential that comprehension instruction be integrated using existing classroom material.

The Key Comprehension Routine is flexible, can be used in all content classrooms, and does not require the purchase of additional instructional materials. Teachers use their knowledge of research-based best practices to teach comprehension using their own classroom materials.

Research also indicates that extensive follow up professional development is necessary in order for teachers to use strategies effectively (National Reading Panel, 2000; Snow, 2002). In order to be successful over the long term, initial training must be followed by further opportunities to practice the application of the training with the support of a professional trainer, a building-based coach, and peer support. The goal is to gradually eliminate the need for a professional trainer.

Professional development for *The Key Comprehension Routine* is provided by Keys to Literacy. This includes initial training, the training of building-based coaches, and on-site follow-up with small groups of teachers when a Keys to Literacy trainer facilitates peer interaction and implementation of the program. The recommended professional development model for implementing *The Key Comprehension Routine* includes the following:

* **Initial Teacher Training:** Using this book, initial training introduces each of the steps in the Routine. Teachers bring classroom reading material to the training so they can practice generating comprehension activities using their own instructional material. At the end of the training, teachers are given implementation portfolios to track their use of the activities. They are encouraged to save examples of classroom comprehension lessons and student work samples in the portfolios to share at follow-up meetings.

* **Training of building-based Key Comprehension coaches:** One or more individuals from a school become peer coaches for *The Key Comprehension Routine*. They attend a Keys to Literacy-sponsored two-day coach training where they learn how to support the implementation of *The Key Comprehension Routine* and assist their peers.

* **Follow-up support for teachers:** A Keys to Literacy trainer conducts small-group meetings at schools. Teachers bring their implementation portfolios and share with their peers the activities and student work from their classrooms. The trainer provides feedback and facilitates the sharing of ideas. If necessary, the trainer reviews the steps, methods, and components of comprehension instruction and offers guided practice. The building coaches attend these meetings so they can learn how to facilitate peer meetings.

＊ **Guided practice sessions:** Guided practice sessions conducted by a Keys to Literacy trainer are also available on-site at schools. During these sessions, teachers have an opportunity to practice generating comprehension lessons and activities with support from the trainer.

For further details about professional development for The Key Comprehension Routine, go to www.keystoliteracy.com or contact Keys to Literacy by email (info@keystoliteracy.com).

NOTES:

Chapter 2

Comprehension Instruction

Comprehension: One of Five Components of Reading

Five areas of instruction must be addressed to successfully teach students to read and comprehend (National Reading Panel, 2000):

* **Phonemic Awareness:** The ability to notice, think about, and work with the individual sounds in spoken words. Before students learn to read, they must understand how the sounds in words work.

* **Phonics:** The ability to understand the relationship between the letters of written language and the individual sounds of spoken language; the use of letter combinations and patterns, syllable types, and word attack skills to read and spell words.

* **Fluency:** The ability to read text quickly, accurately, and automatically, with proper expression and understanding.

* **Vocabulary:** The ability to understand the meaning of words.

* **Comprehension:** The ability to derive meaning based on the information in the text in combination with the reader's own knowledge. Comprehension can be improved by teaching students to use specific reading strategies.

The first three components (Phonemic Awareness, Phonics, and Fluency) are necessary for basic decoding. They collectively allow readers to identify and spell words accurately and fluently. The ultimate goal of reading, however, is to understand what is read. The last two components (Vocabulary and Comprehension) enable readers to construct meaning once words are identified (see Figure A).

Figure A

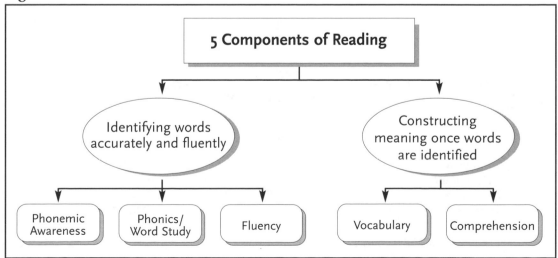

Meta-Cognition

Reading comprehension is a complicated process that requires intentional and thoughtful interaction between the reader and the text. Readers must monitor their understanding, engage in problem-solving, and apply strategies to gain meaning from text. They construct meaning from the combination of information they acquire from the text with their background knowledge. Background knowledge consists of experience with the topic covered in the text as well as knowledge of text structure at sentence, paragraph, and discourse levels (Maria, 1990; Snow, 2002).

Good readers think actively and engage in a process to make sense of what they read. This is referred to as *meta-cognition,* meaning a reader's awareness of himself as a reader and knowledge about the use of strategies. Many poor readers lack this skill. They do not realize what they do not understand, and they have no strategies for making more sense of the text. All students benefit from strategy instruction, but struggling readers in particular need direct, explicit instruction in comprehension strategies to become meta-cognitive. Finally, all students need guided practice with comprehension strategies before they can apply them independently (Carlisle & Rice, 2002; Sweet & Snow, 2003).

What Factors Can Affect Reading Comprehension?

A variety of factors may affect reading comprehension (Biancarosa & Snow, 2004; Jetton & Dole, 2004). Teachers should keep these factors in mind as they attempt to teach comprehension. For some students, instruction in comprehension strategies such as those in *The Key Comprehension Routine* will not be enough to improve comprehension if other factors are not also addressed. Figure B illustrates factors that affect comprehension, along with a brief explanation of each.

Figure B

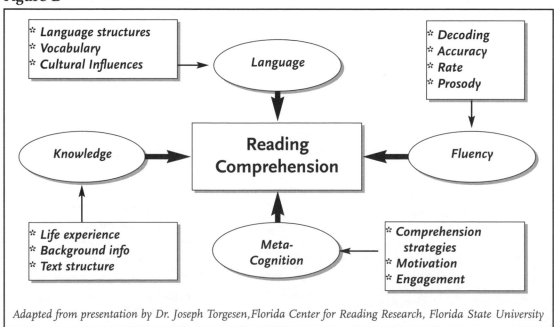

Adapted from presentation by Dr. Joseph Torgesen, Florida Center for Reading Research, Florida State University

Meta-Cognition and Motivation

As noted above, weak self-monitoring skills and a lack of useful strategies can impede reading comprehension. Furthermore, students will be more successful if they are motivated to understand and engage in text they read (RAND, 2002). Instructional practices that improve motivation and engagement in reading include the provision of goals to achieve while reading and opportunities to collaborate with peers to achieve those goals (Guthrie & Humenick, 2004). Teachers can also influence students' motivation by structuring assignments, being attentive to text difficulty, and providing scaffolding for complex text (Moje, 2006; Torgesen, J. K. et al. (2007).

Decoding/Fluency

Research has shown that a core linguistic deficit underlies poor reading at all ages and that poor readers exhibit weaknesses in phonemic awareness, phonics and word attack (decoding), and fluency skills (Shankweiler et al., 1999; Moats, 2001). For many students in grades 4 and up, weaknesses in these areas are the main causes of poor reading comprehension. They devote so much energy and attention to basic reading skill components that they are unable to focus on comprehending what they are reading.

Background Knowledge

A lack of significant life experience and/or vast reading experience can affect the amount of background knowledge a student can access when reading. Without background knowledge of the reading content, students cannot relate to the information sufficiently to construct meaning.

Knowledge of Text Structure

To comprehend, a reader must also have knowledge of text structure at the sentence, paragraph, and discourse levels. Students must be able to understand individual sentences and to link the ideas in a sentence to those in the sentences before and after it. Students who have good grammatical awareness also tend to be good readers (Carlisle & Rice, 2002). Difficult sentences, such as those that contain complicated word order or complex sentence structure, can hinder comprehension. Teachers must be aware of complex sentences in reading they assign and provide scaffolding for students who may struggle with these sentences.

Vocabulary and Language Skills

One of the oldest findings in educational research is the strong relationship between vocabulary knowledge and reading comprehension. Comprehension entails far more than recognizing words and remembering their meaning. However, comprehension is impossible for a student who does not know the meanings of a sufficient proportion of the words in the text (Stahl, 1999; Samuels, 2002).

In addition to a comprehension strategy routine, content literacy instruction should include a routine for teaching vocabulary. *The Key Vocabulary Routine* (Sedita, 2003, 2009) is a professional development program that includes both direct and indirect methods for teaching vocabulary words and vocabulary learning strategies. Information about this program is available at Keys to Literacy's website, www.keystoliteracy.com.

Other Factors

Some students may have additional learning weaknesses that affect comprehension. These may lie in the following areas:

* ✳ Attention
* ✳ Short or long-term memory
* ✳ Visualizing and creating images
* ✳ Expressive language skills
* ✳ English as a second language

What Constitutes Effective Comprehension Instruction?

A complete plan for teaching comprehension should address four components: comprehension strategies, text structure, vocabulary, and background knowledge (see Figure C). *The Key Comprehension Routine* focuses on the first two components (strategies and text structure).

Figure C

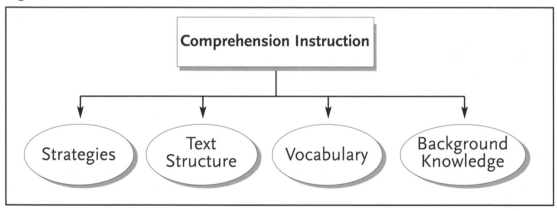

What is Strategy Instruction?

Teaching a relatively small set of comprehension strategies can improve comprehension (National Reading Panel, 2000; Snow, 2002). These strategies are typically used by strong readers, and they include:

* ✳ **Comprehension monitoring.** Readers learn to react if they do not understand, rather than simply continuing to read or skipping over text. Monitoring strategies provide a set of tools that can be used to identify and "fix" misunderstanding while reading.

* ✳ **Use of graphic and semantic organizers (including story maps).** Readers create or complete graphic representations of topics and main ideas in a text, showing how those topics and ideas are related to one another.

* ✳ **Question answering.** Readers answer questions posed by the teacher or by peers and receive immediate feedback on their responses. They determine whether the answer to a question is located in the text or if the answer must be inferred.

✳ **Question generation.** Readers ask questions of themselves or their peer group before, during, and after reading. They learn to consider how these questions fit into a framework of understanding, as in Bloom's Taxonomy (Bloom 1956), and to anticipate test questions.

✳ **Story structure.** Readers use the structure of the story as a means to predict or recall story content in order to retell, summarize, or answer questions about what they have read.

✳ **Summarization.** Readers select and paraphrase the main ideas of text and integrate those ideas into a brief paragraph or several paragraphs that capture the most important ideas in the reading.

✳ **Cooperative learning.** Readers learn and practice strategies together through peer interaction, dialogue with each other, and with the teacher in whole-group activities.

Although each of these strategies is beneficial when used alone, learning is significantly improved when several strategies are combined (Gaskins, 1998; Pressley, 2000; Duke at al., 2004). More specifically, the National Reading Panel (2002) found that strategies can improve results in standardized comprehension tests when used in combination. *The Key Comprehension Routine* incorporates all of the strategies noted above and encourages the combining of two or more strategy activities.

In the 2007 report, *Academic Literacy Instruction for Adolescents* (Torgesen et al.), it is noted that "increasing explicit instruction and support for the use of comprehension strategies is perhaps the most widely cited current recommendation for improving reading comprehension in all studies, particularly for those who struggle with comprehension." (p. 17)

The report also notes that "evidence for the utility of explicit instruction in comprehension strategies has been found not only in controlled experimental studies but also in benchmark studies of more and less effective schools and teachers." (p.18) A number of reviews and syntheses of research offer key information about effective comprehension strategy instruction, from which *The Key Comprehension Routine* was developed. The following are many of the strongest experimental studies and meta-analysis on comprehension strategy instruction:

✳ Lysynchuk, Pressley, and Vye (1990)
✳ Alvermann and Moore (1991)
✳ Dole, Brown, and Trathen (1996)
✳ Klingner, Vaughn, and Schumm (1998)
✳ The National Reading Panel (2000)
✳ The RAND Reading Study Group (Snow, 2002)
✳ Carlisle and Rice (2002)
✳ Meltzer, Smith, and Clark (2003)
✳ Alfassi (2004)

The consensus of opinion is summarized well by Noles and Dole (2004):

> Researchers have collected much evidence that supports explicit strategy instruction ... The teaching of strategies empowers readers, particularly those who struggle, by giving them the tools they need to construct meaning from text. Instead of blaming comprehension problems on students' own innate abilities, for which they see no solution, explicit strategy instruction teaches students to take control of their own learning and comprehension. (p. 179)

Strategy Instruction for Adolescent Readers

Research identifies several specific skills that are particularly effective when teaching reading to adolescent students. Curtis and Longo (1999) describe the reading curriculum for struggling adolescent readers used at the Boys Town Reading Center in Nebraska and replicated in affiliated public schools. Their research found that students made impressive gains in reading (about two years for every year of instruction), and it was possible to bring most of them up to grade level. In addition to instruction in word identification, analysis, fluency, and vocabulary skills, the following comprehension and study skills were most effective:

* Teaching the difference between topics and main ideas

* Teaching that there are many study skills with different functions, and that these tools can be used during both reading and writing

* Teaching the two-column note taking technique

* Teaching mapping, hierarchies, and other kinds of graphic organizers

* Teaching students to generate their own questions during reading, and providing them with the skills to answer these questions

Alvermann and Moore (1991) identified the following specific skills to be especially effective in building independence in reading and studying in adolescent students:

* Rehearsing (underlining, taking notes verbatim)

* Elaborating (taking notes by paraphrasing text, forming mental images, creating an analogy, summarizing)

* Organizing (outlining, mapping)

* Comprehension monitoring (meta-cognitive training, self questioning)

Of these four skills, Alvermann and Moore found that summarizing is generally the most difficult strategy for students to master. However, it becomes easier with explicit instruction over time and scaffolding. All skills noted above are embedded in one or more activities of *The Key Comprehension Routine.*

Writing to Learn

Writing activities have been shown to enhance reading and comprehension. Based on a meta-analysis of the research, Graham and Hebert (2010) found that a cluster of closely related instructional practices are very effective in improving students' reading. These are:

1. Have students write about the texts they read, including writing summaries of text, notes about text, and creating and answering written questions about a text.

2. Teach students the writing skills and processes that go into creating text, including teaching the process of writing, text structures for writing, and paragraph or sentence construction skills.

3. Increase the amount of time students write.

All three findings support *The Key Comprehension Routine*. Activities 2, 3, and 4 of the Routine (two-column notes, summary, and question generation) are exactly the kinds of writing practices identified in Graham and Hebert's research. Chapters 3 (*Main Idea Skills*) and 4 (*Thinking Out Loud, Discussion and Text Structure*) address text structure, in particular at the paragraph level. Finally, the Routine focuses on active learning through frequent discussion and writing.

When Should Strategies Be Taught, and Who Should Teach Them?

Ideally, comprehension instruction should begin as early as grades 1-3. Basic comprehension strategies can be introduced while students are learning beginning reading skills. In grades 4-8, strategy instruction should become a major area of focus as students make the change from "learning to read" to "reading to learn" (Chall, 1996). Strategy instruction should continue during high school as students encounter increasingly more complex text structures and concepts.

Teaching Strategies in the Content Classrooms

Research indicates that teachers who provide comprehension strategy instruction that is deeply connected within the context of subject matter learning, such as history and science, foster comprehension development (Snow, 2002; Biancarosa & Snow, 2004). If students learn that strategies are tools for understanding the conceptual context of text, then the strategies become more purposeful and integral to reading activities. Unless the strategies are closely linked with knowledge and understanding in a content area, students are unlikely to learn the strategies fully, may not perceive the strategies as valuable tools, and are less likely to use them in new learning situations with new text.

Curtis and Longo (1999) note that the ability to practice the strategy with a purpose is even more important than the specific study technique itself. They found that students need numerous opportunities to apply the strategies they are learning and that the practice must occur in situations that are meaningful to students. The research does not show strong results for students who learn skills in isolation and are subsequently expected to apply or transfer those skills appropriately at their own discretion (Meltzer et al., 2003). In their summary of the research on secondary school teaching specific to reading, Alvermann and Moore (1991) concluded that the use of strategies such as taking notes, mapping, and paraphrasing should be built into the curriculum of all content areas and that instilling these strategies is the responsibility of all educators alike.

The Key Comprehension Routine embeds strategy instruction in content classroom lessons using discipline-specific texts and other reading materials.

The Need for Professional Development in Strategy Instruction

A major finding of the National Reading Panel (2000) was that professional development is essential for teachers to develop a knowledge of reading comprehension strategies, to understand which strategies are most effective for different students, and to learn how to teach and model strategy use. In addition, the panel found that teaching reading comprehension at all grade levels is complex. The RAND Reading Study Group (Snow, 2002) noted that recent studies have underscored the importance of teacher preparation as a way to deliver effective instruction in reading comprehension strategies, especially when the students are low-performing.

Some content teachers do not believe that their role includes reading instruction. Many educators, especially content classroom teachers, assume that students have learned to read by the time they reach the 5th grade and that struggling readers need intervention that can only be provided by support staff. Many of the content teachers who are willing to teach comprehension strategies may not know how. Too often, middle and high school teachers have received minimal preservice training in reading instruction; once teachers are in the classroom, opportunities for professional development in content reading instruction are difficult to find. In their report summarizing the research on literacy instruction in middle and high school content areas, Heller and Greenleaf (2007) concluded:

> Perhaps the greatest challenge of all has to do with the scarcity of ongoing, high-quality professional development for teachers. In spite of the many workshops and textbooks dedicated to literacy across the curriculum... relatively few of the nation's secondary school teachers have had meaningful opportunities to learn about the reading and writing practices that go on in their own content areas. More optimistically, though, when they do receive intensive and ongoing professional support, many content teachers find a way to emphasize reading and writing in their classes. (p. 18)

Specifically, "teachers need training in explaining to students when and how to apply strategies, how to model the thinking process and provide examples from classroom lessons, and how to keep students engaged" (National Reading Panel, 2000, p. 16). Quality professional development must be more than individual workshops or training days in order to have a sustainable impact on instruction. From their meta-analysis of effective professional development for teachers, Snow-Renner and Lauer (2005) found that "professional development that is most likely to positively affect a teacher's instruction is:

＊ of considerable duration,

＊ focused on specific content and/or instructional strategies rather than general,

＊ characterized by collective participation of educators (in the form of grade-level or school-level teams), and

＊ infused with active learning rather than a stand-and-deliver model." (p. 6)

The recommended professional development model for implementing *The Key Comprehension Routine* provides in-depth, hands-on training that enables teachers to apply the research on reading comprehension strategy instruction in their classrooms.

NOTES:

Part II

Essential
Comprehension Skills

Chapter 3

Main Idea Skills

The Importance of Main Idea Skills

The ability to identify and state main ideas is a fundamental reading and writing skill. When reading, identifying main ideas helps students avoid getting lost in the details, supports comprehension monitoring strategies, and fosters active learning while reading. In writing, organizing main ideas into a topic web before writing will produce well-constructed compositions and reports. Students must know how to group detail sentences around a main idea in order to produce good paragraphs. When studying, categorizing and storing information by main idea topics and subtopics facilitates the review of information in manageable units.

Categorizing is the most basic application of main idea skills. Grouping items or information by category is a natural way of organizing. Examples in everyday life surround us. For example, department stores display goods according to common categories: men's clothing, women's shoes, towels and linens, etc. Food, dishes, and cooking utensils are stored in kitchen cabinets and drawers by category. The daily newspaper presents stories in sections according to topic: local news, arts and leisure, sports, etc. Some students automatically recognize patterns of organization by category and have a natural tendency to organize their belongings – and the information they learn – this way. Other students do not intuitively develop this skill, especially as it applies to information from reading or class lessons; many need direct instruction in categorizing and other main idea skills before they can apply them independently.

There are various terms used to describe main idea skills, including *chunking, grouping, getting the gist, identifying the topic, theme, topic sentence,* and even *seeing the forest through the trees*. The ability to identify and state a main idea is a fundamental skill for all of the components in *The Key Comprehension Routine*. For example:

❋ In order to create or interpret a top-down topic web, a student must be able to comprehend the relationship between main ideas.

❋ Two-column note taking requires the ability to separate main ideas from details and to determine relevant details that support the main ideas.

❋ Summarizing is particularly reliant on main idea skills because a summary is essentially a restatement of the main ideas in the student's own words.

❋ Question generation, especially at the higher levels of thinking, is often dependent on the ability to go beyond factual details and to apply, analyze, evaluate, or create using the main ideas.

Some students confuse the terms "topic," "main idea," and "topic sentence." *The Key Comprehension Routine* uses the following definitions for these terms:

✳ **Topic:** A broad statement that is often explained using just a few words. Example: the topic of this chapter is *main idea skills.*

✳ **Main idea:** What is being said about a topic, often explained in a phrase or sentence. Example: the main idea of this paragraph is *the difference between the terms topic, main idea, and topic sentence.*

✳ **Topic sentence:** The sentence in a paragraph that includes a statement of the main idea. Often, but not always, the topic sentence is the first sentence of a paragraph. Example: the topic sentence of this paragraph is *Sometimes the terms topic, main idea, and topic sentence can be confusing.*

There is often a hierarchy of topics and main ideas. For example, a reading selection may have one major topic for the whole passage, a few sub-topics, and a number of paragraph main ideas. A textbook chapter might have a single topic, major topics for each section of the chapter, sub-topics that correlate with the bold-faced headings, and paragraph main ideas that support the headings. The graphic organizer used in The Key Comprehension Routine is the top-down topic web, which provides a visual representation for hierarchies of topics.

Start with Examples from Everyday Experiences

While some students have a natural tendency to organize things into categories and information into main ideas, others have great difficulty grasping the concept of main idea. It is helpful to teach main idea skills by providing examples of how we use main idea skills in our day-to-day experiences, such as the examples provided at the beginning of this chapter. When students are asked to apply main idea skills to something with which they are familiar, they can focus on understanding the skill without becoming overwhelmed by new content information.

Activity 1: Practice with Main Ideas

Part 1

Directions: Provide an example from your day-to-day experience of how you use main idea skills. Example: how items are arranged in a grocery store

_____

_____

_____

_____

_____

_____

_____

Part 2
<u>Directions</u>: *What examples might your students give from their day-to-day experience?*
Example: organizing video games

_____

_____

_____

_____

_____

_____

It is also helpful to introduce main ideas using well-organized and structured text before expecting students to apply the skill to complex or disorganized text. If possible, start by asking students to find the main idea of paragraphs that are developed around a single main idea and that only include sentences that support that topic. Ideally, the paragraphs should each have a topic sentence. As students improve their main idea skills, less structured text can be used. School textbooks and other reading material vary significantly in level of structure; sometimes there is even a difference between chapters in the same book. Therefore, students must be taught how to identify and state main ideas from a variety of reading genres and from material that may be unstructured.

A Process for Finding the Main Idea

Teaching main ideas skills can be difficult because there is often no "right answer" – no single best way to state the main idea. Comprehension is influenced by the structure and subject of the text being read as well as the background knowledge, vocabulary knowledge, and overall reading skills of the reader. As a result, decisions about what constitutes the main idea and how to express that understanding are subjective (Snow, 2002). Every reader has a unique combination of experience and prior knowledge about the topic, ability to apply critical thinking, and range of expressive language abilities. The result is that there can be several "correct" answers for identification and statement of a main idea.

In the 1970s, comprehension skill instruction was often based on teaching separate, discrete skills (such as drawing conclusions or finding the main idea) using structured, single-paragraph selections to practice the skill (National Reading Panel, 2000). Students were asked to select the correct answer from several options. However, this approach to teaching main idea skills does not translate to "real life" reading situations where students must identify main ideas using classroom text and generate their own wording to state the main idea. We now know that teaching main idea skills (and other comprehension strategies) using genuine content materials in content classes is the most effective way to improve comprehension (Biancarosa & Snow, 2004).

There is a cognitive process for determining a main idea, and that process can be taught explicitly and directly to students. This process is the same whether a student is categorizing a list of words, identifying the main idea of a paragraph, or identifying a hierarchy of topics in a chapter. The process is as follows:

1. Identify the details.
2. Compare the details to determine what they have in common.
3. Use your own words to paraphrase what they have in common.

Here are some examples:

* Categorizing a list of words: The words are the details. They are compared and a common category is identified, which becomes the main idea. For example, *family members* or *relatives* are examples of main ideas for the words *wife, brother, father, niece, grandmother.*

* Identifying paragraph main ideas: The sentences are the details. They are compared to determine the main idea, which can be stated as a phrase or a sentence. In most paragraphs, the main idea is embedded in a topic sentence, but the main idea may also be implied.

* Identifying the main idea of a section of expository text: The paragraphs are the details, and they are compared to determine the section's main idea. Likewise, the main ideas are the details that are compared to determine the overarching main idea of the entire chapter. For lengthier reading selections, it is important to teach students that multiple levels of main ideas can be organized into a hierarchy. This hierarchy can be represented in a top-down topic web.

* Identifying main ideas from narrative text: The details in the story are compared to determine main ideas relating to characters, setting, theme and other literary elements.

* Identifying the main idea of a science experiment: A series of procedures are followed and observation notes are compared to conclude if the main hypothesis should be accepted or rejected.

* Solving a mystery: The detail clues are compared and analyzed to surmise a solution to the mystery.

As you can see, main ideas are an essential part of everything we learn. Students are typically taught main idea skills as they apply to reading, but main ideas can also be generated from classroom discussions, lectures, and multimedia sources.

Sometimes it is helpful to apply the process noted above in reverse; start with a main idea and then generate details to support that main idea. Whether a student uses a top-down or bottom-up approach to this process, it is important to teach students the relationship between main ideas and details.

Techniques for Finding the Main Idea

It is difficult for some students to understand the concept and find just the right words to state a main idea. The following techniques are helpful for teaching main idea skills.

Goldilocks

The Goldilocks technique is based on the children's story, *Goldilocks and the Three Bears,* in which Goldilocks finds the bears' beds too hard, too soft, and – finally! – just right. Similarly, students often state a main idea too generally or too specifically, but the goal is to state one that is just right. When students use this technique, they ask themselves these questions:

✳ Is my main idea too specific?
✳ Is my main idea too general?
✳ How can I change it to make it just right?

This type of self-questioning helps students develop better main idea statements. The Goldilocks technique can be modeled in class. Ask students to identify the main idea of a paragraph, and record several answers on a board. Through class discussion, have students analyze each statement to see if it needs to be more specific or more general. It will also become apparent very quickly that there is no single best way to state a main idea.

There are some students who may not be familiar with the *Goldilocks* story, or who feel they are too mature to talk about a young child's story. In these cases, other metaphors can be used. For example, a main idea might be described as *too spicy* (too detailed) or *too bland* (too broad).

Figure A provides examples of main idea statements that are too specific, too general, and just right.

Figure A

Paragraph 1:

Bacteria help humans in many ways. Bacteria are involved in the production of food, fuel, medicines and other useful products. Some are used in industry processes. Others help break down pollutants, which are substances such as waste materials or harmful chemicals that dirty the environment.

Main Idea:

    Too specific: Bacteria break down pollutants

    Too general: Bacteria

    Just right: Bacteria help humans in many ways

Paragraph 2:

The first Spanish explorers, such as Coronado, had left horses behind. For a time, bands of horses roamed wild. Then the Native Americans learned to tame the horses and to ride them. As more learned to ride, they moved onto the Plains. With the horse, the Native Americans could easily follow the buffalo herds. Horses also made it easier to chase down and kill buffalo. Because hunting buffalo took far less effort than farming, buffalo became the main food of the Native Americans who lived on the Plains.

Main Idea:

Too specific: <u>Spanish explorers left horses behind</u>

Too general: <u>Horses on the plains</u>

Just right: <u>The use of horses changed life for the Native Americans who lived on the Plains</u>

Labeling the Bucket

A second technique that can be used to help students grasp the concept of a main idea is to use the metaphor of a bucket. Students are shown a picture of a bucket similar to Figure B.

Figure B.

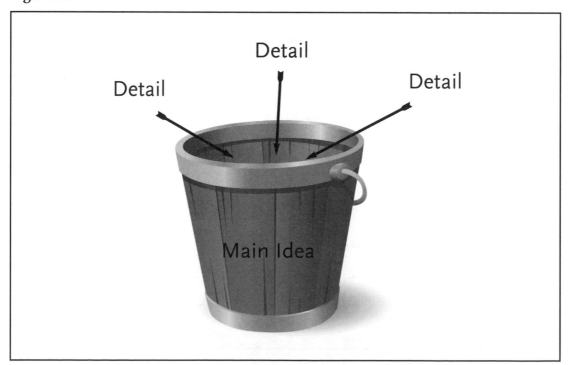

Students are then asked to think about the main idea as if it were a label on the bucket that describes what is inside. This metaphor can be used for basic to more complex levels of main idea skills. For example:

* **Categorizing:** the individual words are the details that go into the bucket, and the label will be the name of the category.

* **Finding paragraph main ideas:** the sentences are the details that go into the bucket, and the label is the main idea of the paragraph. If the label is written in sentence form, it then becomes the topic sentence of the paragraph.

* **Finding the overarching main idea from a multi-paragraph selection:** the paragraphs are the details that go into the bucket, and the label will be the main idea of the selection.

Some students benefit from a demonstration using actual buckets. Other containers such as coffee cups or movie theater popcorn boxes can also be used. To try this activity in your classroom, you will need the following supplies:

* Buckets or containers
* Index cards or small strips of paper
* Lists of words to categorize or paragraphs from a multi-paragraph selection

Directions:

* To practice categorizing, write each word on a card. Ask the students to sort the cards into categories and then place each group of words into a bucket. Students then write a label for the bucket that states the category.

* To practice paragraph main ideas, write individual sentences from a paragraph on strips of paper. Ask the students to place the sentences in a bucket. Students then generate a label that can serve as the topic sentence for the paragraph. Another version of this task is to write the sentences from several paragraphs related to the same topic onto strips of paper, and then mix them up. Ask the students to sort the strips into logical paragraphs and place each group of sentences into a different bucket. Students then label them accordingly.

* To practice the overarching main idea of a multi-paragraph passage, write each paragraph on an index card. On the other side, ask students to state the paragraph main idea. Then have student place the cards in a bucket and compare the various paragraph main ideas to generate a label that reflects the overarching main idea.

Not all students will need this type of hands-on activity to grasp the technique, but the opportunity to actually manipulate words, sentences, and paragraphs is helpful to build basic main idea skills for some students.

Self-Cuing

Self-cuing is a technique that teaches students how to ask themselves a question to help generate a main idea statement. It is especially helpful for paragraphs that have no stated topic sentences. In order to use this technique, students must first identify the general topic of a paragraph or multi-paragraph selection. Then they complete the following to generate a more precise main idea.

The topic is _____.

What is the paragraph saying about the topic? _____.

For example, the topic of the following paragraph is *viruses*. Asking what the paragraph is saying about viruses helps identify the main idea, which might be *viruses cause many types of diseases* or *viruses cause both annoying and serious diseases*.

> Viruses can cause diseases that are annoying and perhaps a bit painful. Some examples of these diseases include colds, fever blisters, and warts. Other diseases caused by viruses are serious and can cause permanent damage or even death. Among the diseases cause by viruses are AIDS, measles, influenza, hepatitis, smallpox, encephalitis, and mumps.

Another type of self-cuing is the *Get The Gist* strategy used in the Collaborative Strategic Reading model, effective in aiding the comprehension of students in grades 4-8 (Klingner, Vaughn, Dimino, Schumm, & Bryant, 2001). In this model, students are taught to answer the following questions to help determine main ideas:

* Name the *who* or *what* the paragraph is mostly about.
* Tell the most important information about the *who* or *what*.
* Write a gist of ten words or less, leaving out details.

The goal for teaching these strategies is to eventually have students independently identify and state main ideas.

Scope and Sequence for Teaching Main Ideas

Systematic instruction means following a sequence that starts with the most basic element of instruction and progresses to more advanced elements. Students gradually build proficiency with a skill as the material and task become more complex. Some students need to be taught main idea skills starting at the simplest level of application, which is categorizing. Even students in middle and high school grades may need to start at this point before they are able to successfully identify main ideas while reading. A scope and sequence for teaching main idea skills in reading is as follows, from basic to complex:

1. Categorize and find the main idea for a list of words.
2. Identify main ideas from paragraphs with topic sentences.
3. Infer and formulate main ideas from paragraphs without a topic sentence.
4. Identify the main idea of a multi-paragraph passage.
5. Identify chapter and section main ideas from textbooks and lengthy reading selections.
6. Practice main idea skills with both narrative and expository text from a variety of subject areas (history, science, language arts, math, etc.).

Suggestions for teaching levels 1-4 listed in the below scope and sequence are provided below. Suggestions for levels 5 and 6 are provided in Chapter 4, *Thinking Out Loud, Discussion, and Text Structure*.

Figure C

A Scope and Sequence for Teaching Main Idea Skills

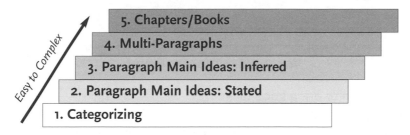

Easy to Complex

5. **Chapters/Books**
4. **Multi-Paragraphs**
3. **Paragraph Main Ideas: Inferred**
2. **Paragraph Main Ideas: Stated**
1. **Categorizing**

Suggestions for Teaching Categorizing

Content-specific vocabulary provides a good source of material to both practice categorizing and develop vocabulary knowledge simultaneously. Categorizing terms into related sub-groups, sometimes called semantic grouping, not only makes them easier to learn (Stahl, 1999), but it is also a good way to practice main idea skills.

To generate a categorizing activity, the teacher identifies a list of words. The teacher can provide the categories and ask students to sort the list into categories; alternatively, students who need less support can determine the categories themselves. Some knowledge of the words is necessary in order to categorize, so it is best to do this activity after words have been previewed or after students have read material containing the words.

For example: Using the words in Figure D, two obvious categories might be *fruits* (apple, banana, grape, orange, pear) and *vegetables* (asparagus, broccoli, spinach, string bean). There may be multiple options for categories. For example, *green food* (apple, asparagus, broccoli, grape, pear, spinach) or *round food* (apple, donut, grape, orange). Some words do not fit into any category, such as *chocolate;* others fall into more than one category (*apple* fits under fruit, round food, and green food). To extend the categorizing activity, ask students to generate additional words associated with the topic that can be added to the categories. Using the category *vegetables,* students might add *carrot* and *squash.*

Figure D

apple	asparagus	banana	broccoli
donut	grape	orange	pear
spinach	string bean	chocolate	

Not all lists of words lend themselves to categorizing. Sometimes there may be only a few words that can be grouped into a category. Word lists that are generated from subject reading such as history, science, or math tend to lend themselves to categorizing, while it might be more difficult to find connections between words from literature.

It is important to note that there are no "right" or "wrong" answers when categorizing words. In fact, students sometimes generate very interesting categories of their own, which provide insight to their general thinking about the topic and the associated words.

Figure E categorizes words from a sixth grade unit on ancient Egypt. As this example illustrates, there can be multiple options for categories, and some words may fit into more than one category.

Figure E

Vocabulary Words: Egypt

amulet: charm worn to bring good luck

Anubis: god of the afterlife

Book of the Dead: a collection of spells/prayers to help with the passage to the afterlife

canopic Jars: containers for the internal organs of an embalmed body

cartouche: oval shape surrounding an inscription of a royal name

cataracts: steep rapids in a river

delta: where the water leaves the river and enters the sea

Giza: the place where the pyramids were built

Hatshepsut: first female ruler of the New Kingdom of Egypt

Imhoptep: the architect who designed the first pyramid for King Zoser

inundation: annual flooding of the Nile

Kush: country to the south of Egypt

Luxor: the place of royal cemeteries

mastaba: rectangular shaped tomb with sloping sides and a flat top

Menes: king who first unified upper and lower Egypt

natron: a mineral/salt used in mummification

obelisk: a tall and thin four-sided stone pillar

papyrus: water reed used for making paper

Pharaoh: title for the ruler of Egypt

Ra: the first, most important Egyptian god

Red Sea: sea that borders Egypt on the east

sarcophagus: a stone coffin

scarab: an amulet in the form of a beetle

scribes: professional writers or record keepers

shroud: a cloth in which a dead body is wrapped

Sphinx: a statue with the head of a human and the body of a lion

tributary: a small river that feeds into the Nile

Possible Categories

People: Hatshepsut, Imhoptep, Menes, pharaoh, scribes

Places: Giza, Kush, Luxor, Red Sea

Objects: amulet, canopic jars, cartouche, papyrus, sarcophagus, scarab, shroud

Words associated with the afterlife: Anubis, Book of the Dead, canopic jars, mastaba, natron, sarcophagus, shroud

Words associated with the Nile River: cataracts, delta, inundation, tributary

Buildings or monuments: Giza, Luxor, mastaba, obelisk, sphinx

Egyptian Gods: Anubis, Ra

Activity 2: Practice Categorizing

<u>Directions</u>: *Review the list of vocabulary words. Create at least two categories that might be used to group some of the vocabulary words. Write the category and the words that support that category on the lines provided.*

Vocabulary Words: Middle Ages

alchemist: a doctor who mixes potions

armor: covering that protects a soldier

chain mail: metal links put together for armor

crusader: Christian soldier

great hall: large gathering place in a castle

guild: a union for trade

jester: a funny performer who provides entertainment to the king

knight: fighter from a noble family

moat: a trench filled with water to protect a castle

nun: religious woman

page: a boy in training to be a knight

serf: a peasant

squire: assistant to a knight

tapestry: a rug on the wall to keep castle rooms warm

Possible Categories

Category 1: _____

Words that support the category: _____

_____

Category 2: _____

Words that support the category: _____

_____

Activity 3: Use Your Content Words

<u>Directions:</u> *Develop a list of at least 10 vocabulary words with their definitions from your content reading. Then identify suggestions for categorizing these words.*

Vocabulary Words

1. _____

2. _____

3. _____

4. _____

5. _____

6. _____

7. _____

8. _____

9. _____

10. _____

11. _____

12. _____

13. _____

14. _____

15. _____

Suggestions for Categories

_____

_____

_____

Suggestions for Teaching Paragraph Main Ideas

A paragraph is the most basic unit of written discourse. In its purest form, the paragraph should consist of several sentences that support one main idea. A contributing factor to successful reading comprehension is the ability to identify paragraph main ideas and then combine and compare those ideas to determine the general theme and concepts from the reading. If students cannot identify paragraph main ideas, reading comprehension is compromised.

As previously noted, the main idea of a paragraph is often stated as a topic sentence. In the early grades, students are taught that the topic sentence will usually be the first sentence in a paragraph. However, as students begin reading more complex text in grades four and up, the topic sentence may also be found in the middle or end of the paragraph. The main idea can also be implied, in which case students must infer it by reading detail sentences and generating their own phrasing to state the main idea. Paragraphs with implied main ideas are more difficult to comprehend than those with explicitly stated topic sentences.

As noted above, it is helpful to introduce main ideas using structured text. A quick review of many middle and high school textbooks reveals paragraphs that contain more than one main idea or a single main idea spread over several paragraphs, as well as paragraphs that contain just a single detail sentence. Sometimes the bold headings in textbooks intended to help students organize their reading do not adequately (or accurately) convey the main ideas. Eventually, students must be taught how to identify and organize main ideas from unstructured reading. When introducing the skill, however, structured text should be used. The best source for text to introduce main idea skills is reading material already being used in class.

Figure F provides examples of paragraphs with a stated main idea in a topic sentence and paragraphs with unstated main ideas that must be inferred.

Figure F

Paragraphs with stated main idea in a topic sentence

<u>History content, expository text</u>

> Many thousands of years ago, the first people to enter the Western Hemisphere came from Siberia in Asia into Alaska in North America. Scientists believe that the two continents were once connected by a land bridge. Today, the waters of the Bering Strait separate Asia from North America. Over long periods of time people crossed the land bridge and spread out over the two American continents and adjacent islands.

> <u>Main Idea:</u> The first people to enter the Western Hemisphere came from Siberia
> <u>Topic Sentence:</u> First sentence

(Reprinted by permission from "American History. 2nd Edition" by Irving. L. Gordon. Revised 1996. Amsco School Publications.Inc. New York, NY)

Science content, expository text

Bacteria help humans in many ways. Bacteria are involved in the production of food, fuel, medicines and other useful products. Some are used in industry processes. Others help break down pollutants, which are substances such as waste materials or harmful chemicals that dirty the environment.

Main Idea: Bacteria help humans
Topic Sentence: First sentence

(Reprinted by permission from "Exploring Life Science" 2nd Edition. 1995. p.143. Prentice Hall (Simon & Schuster Education Group)

Literature, narrative text

That fall Paul Revere did organize a spy system. Thirty artisans, mostly masters, from all over Boston were the center. Each of these men had workmen and apprentices under him. And these had friends and the friends had friends. So this web of eyes and ears multiplied and multiplied again until a British soldier could hardly say he'd like to swim in Yankee blood or a couple of befuddled young officers draw out a campaign on a tablecloth at the Africa Queen but it was reported. It was noted exactly which regiments were on duty in different parts of Boston and how strong were the earth works Gage was putting up to protect his men if 'the country should rush in'.

Main Idea: Paul Revere organized a spy system
Topic Sentence: First sentence

(Excerpt from "Johnny Tremain", by Esther Forbes. Copyright 1943 by Esther Forbes Hoskins; copyright © renewed 1971 by Linwood M. Erskine, Jr., Executor of the Estate of Esther Forbes Hoskins. Reprinted by permission of Houghton Mifflin Company. All rights reserved)

Paragraphs with implied main ideas

History content, expository text

The first Spanish explorers, such as Coronado, had left horses behind. For a time, bands of horses roamed wild. Then the Native Americans learned to tame the horses and to ride them. As more learned to ride, they moved onto the Plains. With the horse, the Native Americans could easily follow the buffalo herds. Horses also made it easier to chase down and kill buffalo. Because hunting buffalo took far less effort than farming, buffalo became the main food of the Native Americans who lived on the Plains.

Main Idea: The use of horses changed life for the Native Americans who lived on the Plains

No Topic Sentence

(From "America's Past and Promise" by Lorna Mason, Jesus Garcia, Frances Powell, C.Frederick Risinger. Copyright © 1995 by Houghton Mifflin Company. All rights reserved. Reprinted by permission of McDougal Littell, a division of Houghton Mifflin Company.)

<u>Literature, narrative text</u>

The bunk house was a long, rectangular building. Inside, the walls were white washed and the floor unpainted. In three walls there were small, square windows, and in the fourth, a solid door with a wooden latch. Against the walls were eight bunks, five of them made up with blankets and the other three showing their burlap ticking. Over each bunk there was nailed an apple box with the opening forward so that it made two shelves for the personal belongings of the occupant of the bunk. And these shelves were loaded with little articles, soap and talcum powder, razors and those Western magazines ranch men love to read and scoff at and secretly believe. And there were medicines on the shelves, and little vials, combs; and from nails on the box sides, a few neckties. Near one wall there was a black cast-iron stove, its stovepipe going straight up through the ceiling. In the middle of the room stood a big square table littered with playing cards, and around it were grouped boxes for the players to sit on.

<u>Main Idea</u>: The bunk house furnishings were meager and sparse
<u>No Topic Sentence</u>

(From "Of Mice and Men" by John Steinbeck. Copyright 1937, renewed © 1965 by John Stenbeck. Used by permission of Viking Penguin, a division of Penguin Group (USA) Inc.)

Activity 4: Identifying Main Ideas

Directions: Read the following paragraphs. Identify the main idea in each paragraph and state it in your own words on the first line. On the second line, note if there is a topic sentence or if the main idea had to be inferred.

Paragraph 1
There was once a town in the heart of America where all life seemed to live in harmony with its surroundings. The town lay in the midst of a checkerboard of prosperous farms, with fields of grain and hillsides of orchards where, in spring, white clouds of bloom drifted about the green fields. In autumn, oak and maple and birch set up a blaze of color that flamed and flickered across a backdrop of pines. Then foxes barked in the hills and deer silently crossed the fields, half hidden in the mists of the fall mornings. *(From "Silent Spring" by Rachel Carson. 1962)*

Main Idea: _____

_____

Topic Sentence: _____

_____

Paragraph 2
During the day, rocks on the Earth's surface are heated by the sun's rays. The outside of the rock heats up and begins to expand. But the inside of the rock

remains cool and does not expand. When the air temperature drops at night, the outside of the rock cools and contracts. The next day, the heat from the sun causes the outside of the rock to expand again. The cycle of heating and cooling continues. Eventually particles on the surface of the rock crack or flake off.

Main Idea: _____

_____

Topic Sentence: _____

_____

Paragraph 3

Graphs are very helpful for displaying data. However, graphs that have been constructed incorrectly can be confusing and can lead to false assumptions. Many times these types of graphs are mislabeled, incorrect data are compared, or the graphs are constructed to make one set of data appear greater than another set. Here are some common ways that a graph can be misleading:

- Numbers are omitted on an axis, but no break is shown.

- The tick marks on an axis are not the same distance apart or do not have the same-sized intervals.

- The percents on a circle graph do not have the sum of 100.

Main Idea: _____

_____

Topic Sentence: _____

_____

Paragraph 4

They lived in a forlorn-looking house that stood alone and had an air of starvation. A few straggling savin trees, emblems of sterility, grew near it; no smoke ever curled from its chimney; no traveler stopped at its door. A miserable horse, whose ribs were as articulate as the bars of a gridiron, stalked about the field, where a thin carpet of moss, scarcely covering the ragged beds of pudding stone, tantalized and balked his hunger; and sometimes he would lean his head over the fence, look piteously at the passer-by, and seem to petition deliverance from this land of famine. (From "The Devil and Tom Walker" by Washington Irving. 1824)

Main Idea: _____

_____

Topic Sentence: _____

_____

Paragraph 5

The Renaissance supported a spirit of adventure and a wide-ranging curiosity that led people to explore new worlds. The Italian navigator Christopher Columbus, who sailed to the Americas in 1492, represented the spirit. So did Nicholas Copernicus, a Polish scientist who revolutionized the way people saw the universe. Renaissance writers and artists, eager to experiment with new forms, were also products of that adventurous spirit.

Main Idea: _____

_____

Topic Sentence: _____

_____

Paragraph 6

The organs in a system depend on each other. If any part of the system fails, the whole system is affected. And failure of one organ system can affect other organ systems. Just think what would happen if your digestive system stopped converting food to energy. One of the other organ systems would not have the energy to function.

Main Idea: _____

_____

Topic Sentence: _____

_____

Paragraph 7

A circle is a round shape with no corners or sides. The distance from the center to any point on its line (circumference) is equal. A wheel, analog clock, and coin are all usually circles. An oval is shaped like an egg – an oblong circle. A square is a shape with four corners and four sides. The length of each side is equal. A sandwich, window, and a tile can be squares. A diamond is a square turned on one of its corners. However, a diamond does not need to have right angles. A kite and a baseball diamond are examples. A rectangle is a shape with four corners and four sides. Each pair of opposite sides has the same length. Most refrigerators, computer screens, and bookcases are rectangles. A triangle is a shape with three corners and three sides. The sides do not have to be the same length, nor do all of the angles need to be the same. A slice of pizza, a sail on a sailboat, and a yield sign are all triangles.

Main Idea: _____

_____

Topic Sentence: _____

_____

Activity 5: Use Your Content

<u>Directions:</u> *Select various paragraphs from your content reading material. Evaluate the structure of the paragraphs to determine if they contain stated or implied main ideas. State the main ideas of each of these paragraphs in your own words.*

Paragraph 1

Stated or Implied? _____

Main Idea: _____

Paragraph 2

Stated or Implied? _____

Main Idea: _____

Paragraph 3

Stated or Implied? _____

Main Idea: _____

Paragraph 4

Stated or Implied? _____

Main Idea: _____

Suggestions for Identifying the Main Idea of a Multi-Paragraph Passage

When students read passages with multiple paragraphs (e.g., newspaper article, supplemental reading from a website, encyclopedia entry), it can be helpful to generate an overarching main idea statement about the passage. At most, this statement should be one or two sentences – it is shorter than a summary. To help students learn to determine a passage's main idea, ask them to follow this progression:

1. Identify the main ideas of each paragraph.
2. Compare these main ideas and determine what they have in common.
3. Develop one or two sentences that state the passage main idea.

As noted earlier, a topic is not the same as a main idea. A topic is the general subject of a paragraph, multi-paragraph passage, or chapter. The topic can usually be stated in 1-3 words. A main idea statement is more specific and tells what is being said about the topic. It is usually easier for students to identify a topic than it is to state a main idea. Where applicable, a title or heading may indicate the topic and provide a clue to the main idea.

Activity 6: Finding the Main Idea of a Multi-Paragraph Passage

<u>Directions</u>: *Read the following selection and identify the paragraph main ideas. Compare these main ideas to create an overarching main idea statement.*

Pirates and Piracy

Pirates are familiar characters. Books and movies like Peter Pan or Treasure Island have romanticized them. But real pirates are criminals, known especially for attacking ships and stealing their cargo while on the high seas. Piracy is different from other types of robbery because it occurs outside the jurisdiction of any one government. Although pirates existed in Roman times and still do today, the ones who inspired the famous images in the movies lived in the 17th and 18th centuries. This era is known as the "Golden Age of Piracy."

The term pirates refers to a general classification of sailors who used their skills to attack other ships. The pirates attacked any ship that seemed to have something worth stealing, whether it was gold, precious cargo, or the ship itself. Unlike other types of pirates, these sailors plundered ships from all nations strictly for their private gain. Bartholomew Roberts, known more commonly as Black Bart, was probably the most successful pirate ever. He captured more than 400 ships in less than four years, traveling the coasts of South America, North America, the Caribbean, and the Bahamas.

A privateer traveled on a ship that carried official papers from a government or company. These papers were called a Letter of Marque. The Letter of Marque gave the ship permission to act on behalf of a specific government or company. For example, if England was at war with Spain, the English government sponsored privateers to attack and plunder the Spanish ships. Theoretically, the Letter of Marque protected the privateers from punishment. But frequently they were tried and punished by nations they were "permitted" to attack. Sir Francis Drake, famous for being the first Englishman to circumnavigate the globe, was a privateer for England. His ship attacked and looted Spanish ships as he traveled in the name of Queen Elizabeth.

Buccaneers were French, English, and Dutch pirates who specifically targeted Spanish commerce ships in the Spanish Main (the coastal areas from northern Florida through the Caribbean and along south America). These pirates differed from privateers because they did not have any state sponsorship. They manned smaller ships than did other pirates, focusing on inlets, bays, and other shallow waters.

Excerpted from Archer, A., Gleason, J., & Vachon, V. (2004). REWARDS Plus: Application to social studies (Student Book) p. 32. Longmont, CO: Sopris West Educational Services.

Paragraph main ideas:

1._____

2. _____

3._____

4. _____

Main Idea Statement:

_____

_____

_____

Finding Main Ideas in Different Content Areas

Each content area has its own set of characteristic literacy practices, and content reading material may vary significantly from one subject to the next (Heller & Greenleaf, 2007). Reading an algebra textbook is very different from reading a chemistry textbook, and both are vastly different from reading literature. The general approaches to identifying main ideas presented in this chapter can be applied to many types of reading. However, it is essential to recognize that there are unique differences in what constitutes a main idea, how it is identified, and how it can be stated – differences determined by subject area and text type. In order to become comfortable finding main ideas in all subject areas, students must spend a lot of time reading and talking about the main ideas in each subject with peers and teachers who will model how to apply strategies.

Some kinds of main ideas and details matter more when reading in history than in science or math. Most math textbooks, for example, do not present information in multiple paragraphs. This does not mean that there are no main ideas or topics/subtopics in math, but rather that text headings and sub-headings are more likely to be a source for identifying main ideas. In science, the reader is often provided with information in graphs, charts, and formulas, from which he must determine the main ideas. In narrative text, main ideas are sometimes developed over several paragraphs or even pages rather than in a single paragraph.

This underscores the need for discipline-specific content teachers to directly and explicitly teach main idea skills, to model the skill using subject-area text, and to provide students with plenty of opportunities for guided practice to apply main idea skills.

NOTES:

Chapter 4

Thinking Out Loud, Discussion, and Text Structure

Good readers think actively and engage in a process to make sense of what they read. This is referred to as *meta-cognition* – meaning a reader's awareness of himself as a reader and knowledge about the use of comprehension strategies. Meta-cognition can also be described as *thinking about thinking*. When students are meta-cognitive while reading, it enables them to tailor their approach to reading to suit text structure.

Content teachers are often in the best position to teach meta-cognition and text structure because they uniquely understand how text is written in their subject area. They also have the best perspective on what reading goals for their discipline should be. After the elementary years, reading assignments become increasingly varied in their style, vocabulary, text structure, purpose, and intended audience. For instance, science textbooks differ from history textbooks, and all textbooks differ from other materials that teachers assign (e.g., newspaper article, primary document, reference material, Internet-based reading). There are numerous genres (e.g., poetry, fable, short story) in English-Language Arts alone.

Developing Meta-Cognition by Thinking Out Loud

A 2008 report from the Institute of Education Sciences (Kamil et al.) made five evidence-based recommendations for educators to improve literacy levels among students in grades 4-12, one of which is providing opportunities for extended discussion of text meaning. As the report explains,

> Teachers should provide opportunities for students to engage in high-quality discussions of the meaning and interpretations of texts in various content areas as one important way to improve their reading comprehension ...Students can, and will, internalize thinking processes experienced repeatedly during discussions. In high-quality discussions students have the opportunity to express their own interpretations of text and to have those positions challenged by others. In the course of an effective discussion students are presented with multiple examples of how meaning can be constructed from text. (pg. 21-22)

A think aloud is an excellent activity for discussion of text meaning and for modeling the components in *The Key Comprehension Routine*. The purpose of a think aloud is to model a thought process for reading difficult material. In a think aloud, the teacher verbalizes his/her thoughts while reading. The most successful applications of strategy instruction involve extended opportunities for discussing texts while students are learning to independently apply strategies, such as generating and answering questions and summarizing (Kamil et al., 2008). When thinking about text meaning is modeled for them, as in a think aloud, students can more readily and easily determine how to use comprehension strategies. The eventual goal is for students to be meta-cognitive independently and automatically.

Thinking out loud and modeling is especially useful for teaching techniques for finding main ideas. The following techniques presented in Chapter 3 lend themselves well to a think aloud:

* ✳ Categorizing
* ✳ The thinking process for finding a main idea
* ✳ Goldilocks
* ✳ Labeling the bucket
* ✳ Self-cuing
* ✳ Identification of stated and implied paragraph main ideas
* ✳ Use of story maps and graphic organizer to represent text structure
* ✳ Use of text heading and sub-headings

Text Structure

Text complexity strongly affects comprehension. Complex or disorganized text structure at the sentence, paragraph, passage, or book level can contribute to difficulty finding main ideas, making connections, and with overall comprehension. It is therefore important for teachers to preview reading material to determine whether text structure will affect comprehension. This does not mean that teachers should avoid having students read complex text – on the contrary. In order to develop adequate literacy skills to succeed in higher grades, post-secondary education, and the 21st-century workforce, students must be exposed to and read significant amounts of complex text. Furthermore, this means that teachers, especially content teachers, need to directly and explicitly teach students how to actively read complex text. Modeling through the use of a think aloud is essential to explicit instruction.

Sentence Level

Sentences that contain complicated word order or numerous phrases and clauses can create comprehension problems. Through the 4th grade, most sentences contain just a simple single or compound subject and predicate. Starting in grade five, however, sentence structure (syntax) becomes more complex. The level of a text's syntax is one predictor of that text's comprehensibility (Snow et al., 2005).

Examples of complex sentence structure:

Many miles downstream on the side to which the dogs had crossed, a small cabin stood near the bank of the river, surrounded by three or four acres of cleared land, its solid, uncompromising appearance lightened only by the scarlet geraniums at the window sills and a bright blue door. (From *"The Incredible Journey"* by Sheila Burnford, ©1960)

Because most Western European countries used imported oil to fuel industries, the higher oil prices caused inflation and slowed economic growth, causing OPEC to again raise prices which triggered a severe recession. (From a middle school social studies textbook)

Recall that the Pythagorean Theorem is often expressed as $a^2 + b^2 = c^2$, where a and b are the measures of the shorter sides (legs) of a right triangle, and c is the measure of the longest side (hypotenuse) of a right triangle. (From a geometry textbook)

Although there are sentence activities to develop proficiency in both reading and writing (e.g., sentence combining and deconstruction, sentence expansion), this instruction tends to be limited to English-Language Arts or reading/writing classes. While it is not practical for other content teachers (i.e., social studies, science, math) to teach sentence grammar, it is helpful to review complicated sentences and model the construction of meaning before students are asked to independently read such texts.

Paragraph Level

Chapter 3 reviewed the structure of a basic paragraph. We also noted that all texts do not contain well-written paragraphs. Many students become overwhelmed by details when they read more than a few paragraphs. If a teacher determines that some students may have difficulty identifying paragraph main ideas, the following scaffolding activity can be used.

Before students read, preview the text and determine if each paragraph has a topic sentence or if the main idea must be inferred. Place the following letter clues in the margin next to each paragraph.

B   If the main idea is located at the beginning of the paragraph.

M   If the main idea is located in the middle of the paragraph.

E   If the main idea is located at the end of the paragraph.

I   If the main idea is implied.

A main idea can be stated in the first sentence (as a topic sentence) and repeated in the last sentence (as a concluding sentence). When this occurs, two letter clues (**B** and **E**) can be provided to indicate that the main idea is repeated. Letter clues allow the teacher to offer some assistance, but students must still identify the main ideas. Another option is to underline topic sentences or provide main ideas in the margin next to paragraphs without stated main ideas.

When text contains poorly structured paragraphs, visual clues such as brackets or arrows can be helpful. For example: One paragraph may contain two main ideas, or one main idea may be spread out over several paragraphs. In this case, a bracket can be used to combine or break apart the paragraphs. A paragraph may also contain a detail sentence that supports the main idea of a different paragraph. In this case, using an arrow to connect that sentence to another paragraph may be helpful. Figure A is an example of how letter clues, underlining of main ideas, and a visual clue (bracket) are applied to a passage from a history textbook.

Figure A

The Red Scare Begins

B Many <u>Americans had been deeply disturbed by</u> the Bolshevik victory in the Russian Revolution of 1917 and the subsequent <u>spread of communism</u>. German Communists were able to hold the city of Berlin for a few days in 1919. For five months Communists ruled Hungary, which had regained its independence from Austria following the First World War. Communist sympathizers in the United States and western Europe seemed to many people to have great power. The labor turmoil alarmed people who feared that America, too, was turning radical.

M During the First World War, moreover, people had been made suspicious of anything "un-American". Those old <u>suspicions were now revived, this time with Communists in mind</u>. For instance, the chief speaker for the coal operators declared, without any evidence, that the coal strike was financed by Bolshevik gold on direct orders of the Russian leaders. This feverish suspicion of Communist revolutionaries became known as the "Red Scare."

B <u>Americans were further distressed by a number of acts of terrorism</u>. One involved Mayor Ole Hanson of Seattle. Hanson had gained nationwide publicity when he had called on troops to break up a strike of shipyard workers in February, 1919. Soon afterward he received a bomb in the mail. Fortunately, the bomb was found before anyone was hurt.

Other terrorist incidents followed. Senator Thomas Hartwick of Georgia, a well-known anti-Communist, received in the mail a bomb that did explode, injuring the maid who opened the package. Another bomb destroyed the home of Attorney General A. Mitchell Palmer. During the spring and summer of 1919, postal authorities discovered more than thirty bombs addressed to citizens known to be opposed to organized labor or unrestricted immigration.

B The <u>high point of tension</u> came on September 16, 1920, <u>when a bomb exploded on Wall Street at noon</u>, killing more than thirty people and injuring hundreds of others. Palmer's opinion that Communists were preparing "to rise up and destroy government at one fell swoop" was widely accepted as true.

B Beginning in the fall of 1919, <u>Palmer</u>, a zealous man, <u>led law-enforcement agencies in a series of raids against suspected Communists</u>. Over 6,000 people were arrested, and about 550 of them were deported. During the "Red Scare", even governmental officials were not immune from attacks on their civil liberties. In New York in 1920, five Socialists who had been legally elected were denied their seats in the state legislature.

(From "America, the Glorious Republic", Revised Edition by Henry F. Graff. ©1990 by Houghton Mifflin Co. All rights reserved. Reprinted by permission of McDougal Littell, a division of Houghton Mifflin Co.)

Text Level

Students must learn that there is a significant difference between narrative and expository text: Narrative text tells a story, while expository text explains or gives factual information.

Narrative text typically includes basic literary elements such as setting, characters, a problem and its solution, a theme, and a series of events. Main ideas in narrative text therefore tend to be main events that can later be used to develop a plot summary.

Teaching story structure helps students identify and answer main idea questions such as *who, what, where, when,* and *why* about the plot, characters, and events in stories (National Reading Panel, 2000). Students begin learning story structure before they even enter school via exposure to countless stories (oral or written) and hearing fluent reading. A story map is a visual representation, or graphic organizer, of the story structure (Beck & McKeown, 1981); it should reference the major components of a narrative text. Story maps provide an organizing framework that helps focus attention on the important information in the story, and the ability to use this knowledge to aid comprehension continues to improve with age (Williams, 2002). Please refer to the sample story maps in Figure B on pages 50 and 51.

Expository text, the most common type of text used in content classes, is always nonfiction and explains information. Not surprisingly, expository text is the structure most often found in textbooks. It tends to be structured around a hierarchy of main ideas, ranging from broad topics represented by chapter and section headings to paragraph-level main ideas.

Research supports the use of graphic organizers to represent the relationships between underlying ideas in expository text. Several studies of students in grades 4-6 suggest that teaching students to organize ideas from reading in a systematic, visual graph improves their ability to remember what they read. More generally, it may also transfer to better comprehension and achievement in social studies and science content areas (National Reading Panel, 2000). *The Key Comprehension Routine* employs a top-down topic web organizer as an especially useful strategy before, during, and after reading expository text. (See Activity 1, *Top-Down Topic Web.*)

Most textbooks include unit and chapter titles, section headings, and sub-headings that generally identify the main ideas well. However, some longer reading selections do not provide headings, and sometimes the text is not well-organized. Teachers should provide direct instruction, including modeling, for how titles and headings can be used to organize the information in text. If the reading is not structured, the teacher should scaffold the text by adding new or better headings and/or providing a list of main ideas or a graphic organizer. In order to provide this kind of scaffolding, teachers must preview reading assignments to determine how much structure is provided and how readily the main ideas can be discerned.

Figure B

Story Map	
Title and Author	
Main Characters	**Setting**
Supporting Characters	**Problem**
Solution	

Story Map

Title: _____

Author: _____

Setting

Characters

Problem

Major Events

    1. _____

    2. _____

    3. _____

    4. _____

    5. _____

    6. _____

Solution

Activity 1: Use Your Content

Using reading material from your content classroom, select a section of text. Try to select text that contains at least five paragraphs. If you are using a math textbook, select a short chapter or section of a chapter. If you are using narrative text such as a short story or novel, select the first few pages of a chapter.

Part 1: Review The Structure

Directions: Review your reading selection and answer the following questions.

Overall Structure:

❇ Are there headings and subheadings?

_____

_____

❇ If so, do they provide an accurate description of the main ideas?

_____

_____

❇ Do you think it would help students to add headings or provide different wording for the headings?

_____

_____

Paragraph Structure:

❇ If there are paragraphs, are they well-structured (i.e., is there one main idea per paragraph)?

_____

_____

❇ Are the main ideas stated in topic sentences or implied?

_____

_____

Sentence Structure:

❇ Are there any sentences so complex as to affect comprehension?

_____

_____

Part 2: Identify Main Ideas and Details

<u>Directions</u>: *Practice underlining or highlighting main ideas and key supporting details in the text. If the main ideas are implied, write them down in the margins. (If you cannot write in the book, use pencil so you can erase.)*

Part 3: Practice Modeling and Think Aloud

<u>Directions</u>: *Identify ways that you could have an extended discussion about this text with students to model comprehension while reading. Incorporate any of the scaffolding techniques provided in Chapter 3 and earlier in this chapter. Then work with a partner to model a think aloud of your text.*

Part III

The Four Activities in
The Key Comprehension Routine

Activity 1

Top-Down Topic Web

Research supports the use of graphic and semantic organizers to represent the relationships between the underlying ideas in text. Teaching students to organize ideas in a systematic, visual graph improves their ability to remember what they read (Klingner & Vaughn, 2004). More generally, the use of graphic organizers also contributes to better comprehension and achievement in the content areas, such as social studies and science (National Reading Panel, 2000).

There are a plethora of graphic organizers that can be used to represent various types of text structure. For example, a pair of overlapping circles can be used to represent like and unlike features for a compare and contrast (see Figure A). Another commonly used graphic organizer is a brainstorming web. This is often used to generate ideas about a topic before reading or writing (see Figure B).

Figure A

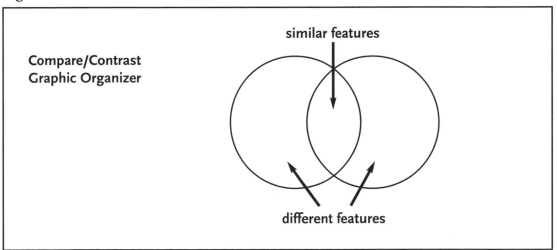

Figure B

However, the availability of so many different types of graphic organizers often results in confusion about when and how to use them. As they move from class to class and encounter teachers using different kinds of graphic organizers, students become overwhelmed and tend to focus more on figuring out how to use each new template instead of how to generate their own graphic organizer to help learn information. The first activity in *The Key Comprehension Routine* is the top-down topic web, a fundamental graphic organizer (see Figure C). It is flexible enough to suit the material in any content area. This does not mean that teachers should not use other types of graphic organizers. Rather, the top-down topic web should be used as a standard graphic organizer to promote its consistent use across all subjects, complemented by other graphic organizers for more specific (and, as necessary, content-specific) purposes.

Figure C

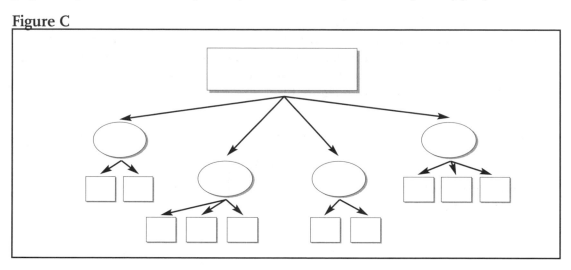

Many students become overwhelmed by too much information, focus excessively on details, and lose sight of the big picture when they read. *The Key Comprehension Routine* topic web provides a clear visual overview of the main ideas. As illustrated in Figure C, levels of topics and sub-topics are arranged in a top-down format. The overarching topic is placed at the top, and the sub-topics are arranged vertically to represent the relationship of each topic to the others in a hierarchy.

Use of Position, Shape, and Color

Both the placement of topics in the web and the use of shape and color (when available) play an important role in making a top-down topic web user-friendly to students because they visually accentuate the relationships between topics. Follow these guidelines to generate a top-down topic web:

 ✳ Place the broadest topic at the top of the web, sub-topics beneath those, and more subordinate sub-topics towards the bottom of the page.

 ✳ Use different shapes to denote the level of the topic. For example, the broadest topic at the top might be in a rectangle, the sub-topics in circles, and the subordinate sub-topics in diamond shapes. While the choice of shape does not matter, the consistent use of the same shape for each level does. For example, two shapes (rectangle, oval) alternate levels in Figure A.

✳ Use arrows to accentuate the connections between the topics.

Stacking

If there is enough room on the page, it is best to keep topics at the same level (and shape) along the same vertical line of the topic web. However, that is sometimes not possible because of limited space. If necessary, topics at the same level can be stacked. Figure D shows stacked subordinate topics (rectangles) under the three sub-topics (ovals).

Figure D

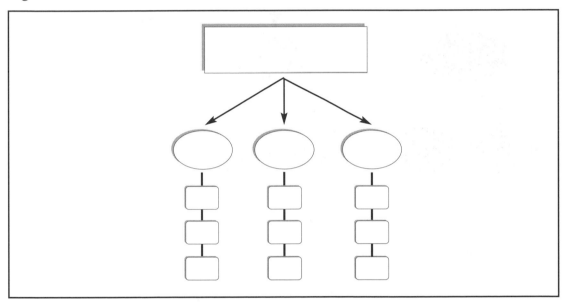

When topics are stacked, it is best to use a line to connect items (rather than an arrow). This will help visually reinforce that the stacked items of the same shape are equally subordinate to the broader sub-topic.

Using Color

Color can be used to further emphasize the relationship between ideas in a web. Color can be used in two ways:

✳ vertically: same color for one topic and all of its sub-topics

✳ horizontally: same color for all the sub-topics on one level, different color for all the subordinate sub-topics on a lower level

Figure E illustrates both ways of using color.

Figure E

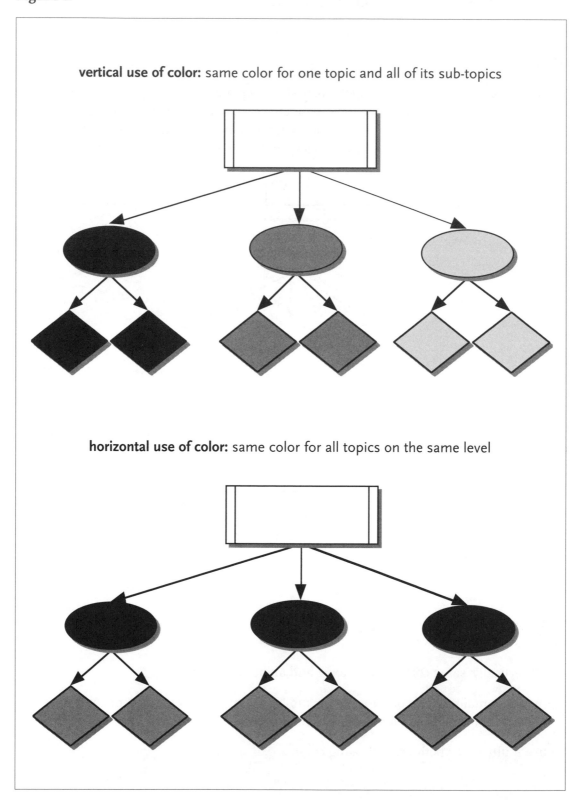

Sources of Information for Generating Top-Down Topic Webs

When a textbook chapter is the basis of instruction, a top-down topic web can be generated from the headings and sub-headings in the book or the paragraph main ideas. Figure E provides an example of a top-down topic web generated from a science textbook chapter. Figure F was generated from the passage on page 41 about pirates, and Figure G was generated from the passage on page 48 about the Red Scare.

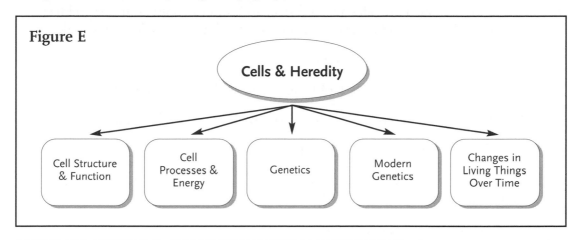

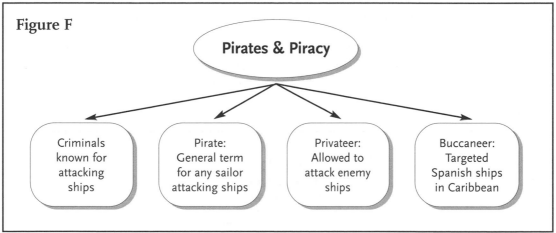

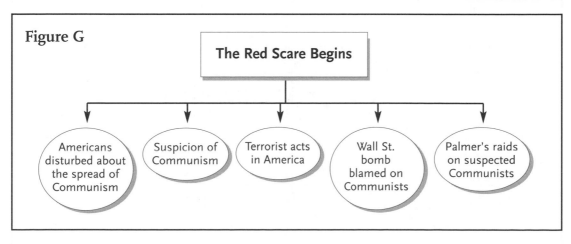

In addition to topics from reading, a top-down topic web can also be used to represent information and concepts from a variety of other sources. For example, it is helpful to use a web to introduce the main topics that will be covered during a whole semester. Students often have difficulty connecting material taught from day to day and week to week; a top-down web provides an overview before, during, and after instruction to help students make these important connections. Teachers often discover that the development and use of these topic webs helps keep their lessons organized and focused, and the web also provides a useful structure for developing quizzes and tests. Some examples of sources other than textbooks for developing a topic web include:

* The main events of someone's life from a biography

* Literary elements from a work of fiction (e.g., setting, characters, plot)

* Major concepts addressed through a series of science experiments

* Model for studying elements of poetry

* Organizing components of a foreign language unit (e.g., vocabulary, grammatical rules)

* Main points from a classroom lecture

* Essential questions or items from state-wide curriculum frameworks

Several classroom examples of top-down topic webs from various subject areas are provided at the end of this book. Figure H is a topic web developed from the Massachusetts Social Studies Curriculum Framework, *Mesopotamia and the Fertile Crescent*.

Figure H

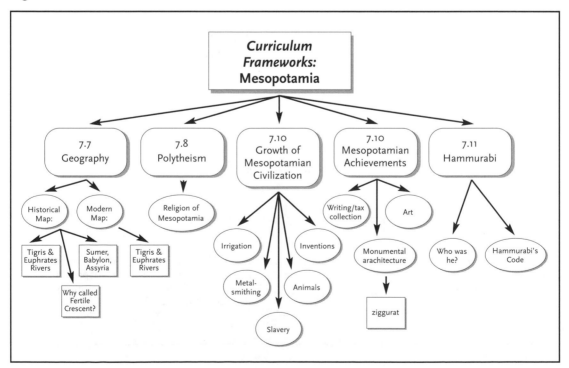

Turning a Segment of a Top-Down Topic Web Into a Sub-Web

Sometimes it is necessary to provide more detail to a topic web than can reasonably fit in a single web. More detail can be easily accommodated by developing a segment of a web into another, separate sub-web. Figure I is a topic web that was generated from a science unit about organic compounds. The first segment of that web (carbohydrates) has been developed into a more detailed sub-web.

Figure I

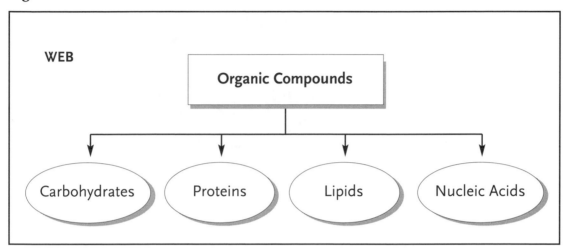

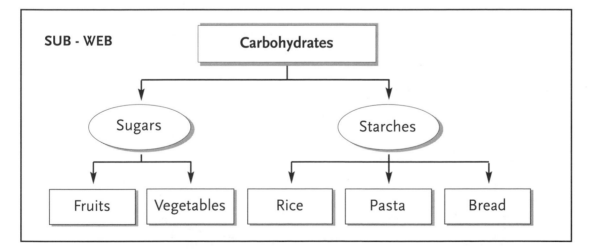

Teacher- and Student-Generated Topic Webs

Until students can develop webs independently, teachers need to generate and provide examples of topic webs. Even though students can become proficient at creating webs in one year, they will still need teacher-generated examples as they progress through higher grades where material is more challenging. Also, students will learn and master strategies at different rates. Teachers can scaffold their instruction by providing webs at various stages of completion to meet different student learning needs. Figure J illustrates three stages of a topic web that was developed for a fifth-grade introduction to geometry. The first is a blank template – students must determine all of the topics;

in the second, students must provide some of the topics; and the third is a completed web that might be used with struggling learners.

Figure J

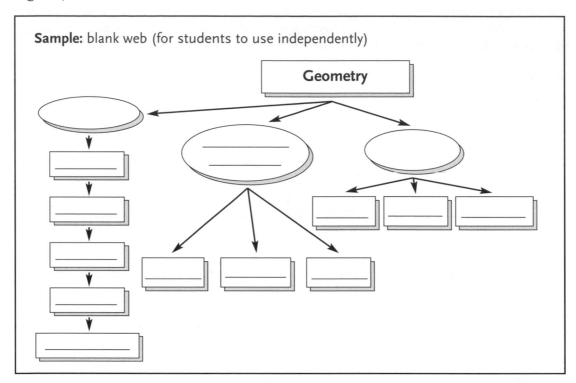

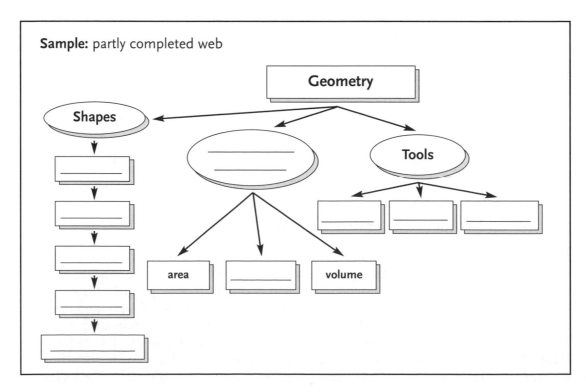

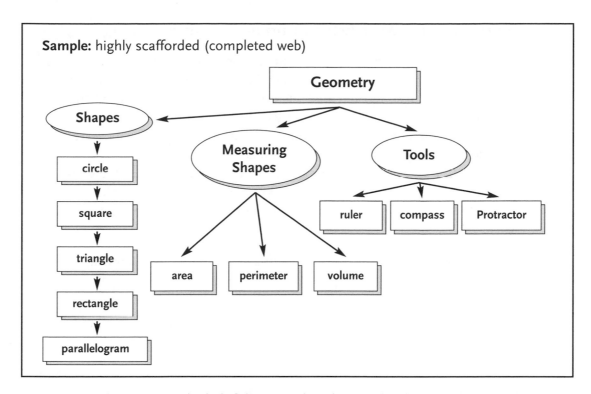

Sample: highly scaffolded (completed web)

For some students, it may be helpful to introduce how to develop a top-down topic web by asking them to generate one by organizing something they are already familiar with (e.g., organizing their video games or sports equipment). See Figure K.

Asking students to generate top-down topic webs in small groups is a good way to help them become independent in the development of these graphic organizers. Allowing students to discuss what they think are the important topics and sub-topics and how to best represent them provides an opportunity for peer think-aloud and extended discussion of text.

Figure K

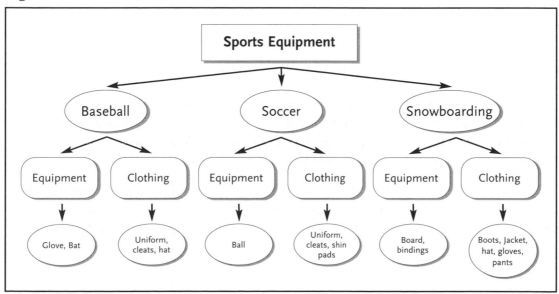

Using Top-Down Topic Webs Before, During, and After Reading

When used as a previewing activity before reading, a topic web enables students to set goals and to activate their background knowledge. Previewing helps determine where to focus attention during reading, and students understand text more fully when given previews (Brody, 2001). Before reading, a topic web helps students recognize the structure and organization of the text and enables them to create a mental overview of the information. As noted above, topic webs can also be used to introduce a unit of study. To activate prior knowledge, the teacher can ask students to review the items in the topic web and think about what they already know about these topics. Next, students should turn the topics into questions or make some predictions about what they think they will learn.

Before you introduce a new unit of study or reading selection, do the following:

1. Develop a top-down topic web that represents the major ideas.

2. Have students review the web in order to see the big picture of what they will learn.

3. Ask students to identify at least one item on the web about which they have some prior knowledge, and have them write that information down.

4. In small groups or class discussion, have students share that information.

5. If students have inaccurate background knowledge, be sure to correct and/or clarify the information.

6. Ask students to choose at least one item on the web to generate a question they would like answered or to make a prediction about what they think they will learn.

7. In small groups or class discussion, have students share their questions and predictions.

During reading, the construction of mental representations in memory enhances comprehension. Those mental pictures involve not only descriptive images, but also representations of relationships between ideas. Such mental images help students to understand the processes or events in the text as well as remember more abstract concepts (Gambrell & Bales, 1986). It is important to review the topic web again during reading or throughout a unit of study in order to help students understand how details fit in with the big picture. A topic web essentially pieces information into manageable units to be learned in sections and then joined together again in the big picture puzzle.

Finally, a topic web is a helpful after-reading strategy. It serves as a general study guide, enabling students to once again step back to the big picture. The topics and sub-topics identify specific units to study for a test instead of an overwhelming list of details.

Using Top-Down Topic Webs to Organize Before Writing

While *The Key Comprehension Routine* emphasizes top-down topic webs to support comprehension, webs can also be used to organize information before writing. When writing about content from reading, the topic web organizes big ideas that can then be used to generate a summary. A topic web can also be used to organize details from research notes into sections for a research report. Finally, ideas for writing can be brainstormed and then organized into a top-down topic web to organize the ideas into sections and paragraphs for an essay or report.

Activity 1: Create a Top-Down Topic Web

Directions: Using classroom reading material or content from a unit of study you will teach, generate a top-down topic web.

Activity 2: Create a Sub-Web

<u>Directions</u>: *Using a segment of the top-down topic web you generated, develop a sub-web that includes another level of detail.*

Activity 2:

Two-Column Notes

Note taking is a procedure for recording information from reading, lectures, or class lessons. When students take notes, comprehension is enhanced as they process, organize, and restate the information in their own words. Note taking boosts meta-cognition as students actively search for main ideas and key supporting details, and it is also a valuable tool for gathering and organizing information for a report or research paper. Note taking instruction can be introduced as early as second and third grade, but it should be a major focus of instruction in the middle school grades.

Taking notes, especially from lectures, is a difficult task for many students, because it requires the integration of auditory processing skills, visual-motor skills, writing skills, reading or listening comprehension skills, and sustained attention. Taking notes from reading is easier, because students can read portions of the text several times at their own pace. As such, note taking from reading should be introduced and practiced before students are expected to take notes independently from lectures.

Two-Column Format

To take notes, students must identify main ideas and key details, paraphrase them using as few words as possible, and record them in a structured format. In the late 1970s, Joan Sedita and her colleagues at Landmark School in Massachusetts developed a two-column format adapted from Walter Pauk's Cornell System for taking notes (Sedita, 1989, 2001; Pauk, 1997). The format is described below and illustrated in Figure A.

To begin, a page of two-column notes should have a vertical line drawn down the length of page and a horizontal line intersecting it near the top (to form a "T" shape). As shown in Figure A, the vertical line is approximately one third of the way across the page from the left border. This two-column format provides a clear visual distinction between main ideas (to be listed in the left column) and key details (right column). A heading or topic should be noted at the top of the page.

The two-column note format has several advantages over outlines. First, the layout is simple and provides a stronger visual distinction between main ideas and details: they are separated by a vertical line. In a traditional outline format, there are only small indentations to denote the difference between main ideas and details; especially when outlines are written by hand, the spacing may be inconsistent. The result is often pages of notes that appear as a steady stream of words, making it more difficult to later review and study the notes. Furthermore, outlining requires students to be attentive to irrelevant information – for example, whether they should use capital or small letters and Roman or Arabic numerals as they list information in an outline.

The two-column format is also efficient for studying. The details in the right column can be covered as the student reads each main idea and quizzes himself on the details. Likewise, the left column can be covered as the student uses the details to test his knowledge of the main ideas.

Figure A

Heading or Topic of Notes	
Main Ideas	**Details**

Detailed Notes versus Big Picture Notes

Regardless of whether students take notes from reading or a lecture, they typically must record all of the main ideas and supporting details. Main ideas tend to come directly from paragraph main ideas or topic sentences, and the details are usually the supporting sentences. Figure B is notes taken from sample paragraphs used in Chapter 3, and Figure C is notes taken from the passage in Chapter 4 on page 48, *The Red Scare Begins*.

Figure B

Paragraph:

Bacteria help humans in many ways. Bacteria are involved in the production of food, fuel, medicines, and other useful products. Some are used in industry processes. Others help break down pollutants, which are substances such as waste materials or harmful chemicals that dirty the environment.

Notes:

Bacteria

Bacteria help humans	- involved in food, medicines, fuels - used in industry processes - break down pollutants (waste materials or harmful chemicals)

Paragraph:

The bunk house was a long, rectangular building. Inside, the walls were whitewashed and the floor unpainted. In three walls there were small, square windows, and in the fourth, a solid door with a wooden latch. Against the walls were eight bunks, five of them made up with blankets and the other three showing their burlap ticking. Over each bunk there was nailed an apple box with the opening forward so that it made two shelves for the personal belongings of the occupant of the bunk. And these shelves were loaded with little articles, soap and talcum powder, razors and those Western magazines ranch men love to read and scoff at and secretly believe. And there were medicines on the shelves, and little vials, combs; and from nails on the box sides, a few neckties. Near one wall there was a black cast-iron stove, its stovepipe going straight up through the ceiling. In the middle of the room stood a big square table littered with playing cards, and around it were grouped boxes for the players to sit on.

Notes:

Housing for the Workers

Bunk house furnishings were meager and spare	- plain walls and floor - small windows - bunks with burlap blankets - old apple boxes for shelves - stovepipe through the ceiling - one table with boxes for chairs

Figure C

The Red Scare Begins

Americans disturbed about spread of communism in Europe	- Bolsheviks win in Russian Revolution - communist sympathizers in U.S. - labor problems turning radical
Suspicion of communists	- Americans suspicious since WWI - known as the Red Scare
Terrorism in America	- Mayor Hanson of Seattle breaks up strike then receives mail bomb - Senator Hartwick receives mail bomb - bomb destroys Attorney General Palmer's home - 30 mail bombs discovered
Wall Street bomb blamed on communists	- high point of tension - 30 people killed
Palmer's raids on suspected communists	- law enforcement raids on suspected communists - over 6000 arrested, 550 deported - even government officials lost civil liberties

Sometimes, however, it is not efficient to take detailed notes – especially when reading multiple pages, such as a full chapter in a textbook. Here, students should switch to big picture notes. Instead of placing paragraph main ideas in the left column and sentence details in the right column, the student should place section main ideas in the left column and paragraph main ideas in the right column. Boldface headings in textbook chapters can be used to generate the left-column main ideas. When taking big picture notes, it is helpful to stop every few paragraphs to think and consider how the paragraph main ideas relate to the text that comes before and after.

Please refer to the classroom examples of detailed and big picture two-column notes from various subject areas at the end of this book.

Teaching Note Taking

It is essential that teachers focus on teaching students the underlying skills needed to take notes rather than simply showing them the two-column format. At all grade levels, it is also important for students to take notes independently, rather than copy them. It is the combination of thinking <u>while</u> taking notes that enables students to become active readers and listeners, which is ultimately the only way they retain essential content information.

A combination of modeling and thinking aloud by the teacher and practice in small collaborative groups is helpful. For example:

* The class reads a text selection as a group.

* The teacher then asks the students to identify main ideas and details and writes them on the board, overhead transparency, SMART board, etc.

* Students practice taking notes in small groups.

Meta-cognitive skills are reinforced as students think aloud to identify important main ideas and details and state the information succinctly in their own words.

Scaffolding Notes to Differentiate Instruction

In order to meet the needs of students with a wide range of note taking abilities, teachers can provide several versions of a single set of notes:

* **A blank template.** Students identify all the main ideas and key details.

* **A partially completed template.** The teacher provides the main ideas, and the students identify the details (or vice versa).

* **A complete set of notes.** To assist struggling readers, the teacher provides a completed set of notes.

Figure D illustrates these three different levels of scaffolding.

Figure D

Sample: highly scaffolded notes

Section 1: Discovering Cells

Cells	• Basic units of structure and function in living things • Building blocks of _____ • People are made of _____ • Too small to see

First sightings of cells	• 1590 microscope invented
	• Microscope = _____
	• Robert _____
	  o 1st to see cells in _____
	  o saw cells in _____
	• Anton van _____
	  o Same time as Hooke
	  o Saw organisms in _____
	  o Saw_____ in scrapings from _____

Microscope improvements	• 1590: 1st M – tube with _____ _____ _____ • 1660: Compound M – _____shines light • 1683: Leeuwenhoek's M – first to see tiny_____ • 1886: Compound Light M –_____focuses light • 1993: Transmission Electron M – sends _____ through dead specimens to make image • 1965: Scanning Electron M – beam of electrons _____ a specimen • 1981: Scanning Tunneling M – electrons that _____from surface of specimen.

Cell Theory	• All living things are _____
	  o Schleiden concluded – all _____ are made of cells
	  o Schwann concluded – all _____are made of cells
	• They didn't know _____
	• Cell theory developed
	  o All living things – composed of _____
	  o Cells – basic unit of_____ and _____
	  o Produced from _____
	• Theory is true for all _____things

How a light microscope works	• _____ properties:
	• Magnification: ability to _____
	  o Lenses bend _____that passes through them
	  o Convex Lens = lens with _____
	  o Compound M uses more than _____lens & can magnify more
	• Resolution: ability to _____
	  o Same as _____
	  o Good resolution = _____

Electron Microscopes	• Since 1930's • Use beam of electrons instead of _____ • Electrons – tiny, smaller than _____ • Resolution is much _____

Sample: somewhat scaffolded notes

Section 1: Discovering Cells

Cells	• Basic units of structure and function in living things • • •

First sightings of cells	• 1590 microscope invented
	• Microscope = _____
	• Robert _____
	   o
	   o
	• Anton van _____
	   o
	   o
	   o

Microscope improvements	• 1590: • 1660: • 1683: • 1886: • 1993: • 1965: • 1981:

Cell Theory	• All living things are _____
	   o Schleiden
	   o Schwann
	•
	• Cell theory developed
	   o
	   o
	   o
	• Theory is true for all _____things

How a light microscope works	• _____ properties:
	•
	   o
	   o
	•
	   o

Electron Microscopes	• Since 1930's • • •

Sample: for students who can take independent notes. They can also be given a blank piece of paper.

Section 1: Discovering Cells

Cells	
Microscope improvements	
How a light microscope works	

Note Taking Sub-Skills

In order to be efficient note taker, students must develop three sub-skills:

* Abbreviating
* Paraphrasing using concise wording
* Using visual cues to edit notes

Many middle and high school students do not know how to properly use abbreviations in notes. Teachers should provide direct instruction and model how to use abbreviations while taking notes. They should demonstrate how abbreviations can be generated from the first syllables in words (e.g., "Eng" for England; "Ren" for Renaissance) and meaningful parts of words (e.g., condemn for condemnation); many students may also need direct instruction in commonly accepted abbreviations (e.g., "w/" for with, "+" for and). While modeling note taking, teachers can also ask students to suggest abbreviations.

Paraphrasing main ideas and details into concise phrases is another essential sub-skill for note taking. It is ironic that by grade 5, when students have finally learned to write in complete sentences, they must then learn to write only short phrases for note-taking. Teachers can model paraphrasing by thinking aloud and reviewing their decisions about word choice. Students need significant practice with this skill to become proficient paraphrasers.

Finally, some students need direct instruction in how to add visual markers to better organize notes on a page. This can be done when notes are edited and reviewed. Some examples of visual markers include:

* Draw horizontal lines across the page after each main idea to clearly "chunk" the notes.

* Use colored markers to highlight important information or to make connections between sections of notes that are related.

* Number the order of details.

* Leave extra space after each main idea so there is room to add information that may have been missed.

* Add arrows, stars, or brackets to show connections between ideas.

Without proper note taking instruction, some students may write down everything they read or hear from a lecture. Some believe that longer notes translate to a better grade. Students must learn that note taking is a specific kind of writing task; as they move into upper grades where they will take notes from large volumes of reading, sometimes "less is more." Teachers need to differentiate their note taking instruction to teach some students how to write less and others to write more.

Note *Taking* Versus Note *Making*

Note taking entails recording information in an organized format, such as two-column notes. Note making is the application of active strategies for learning and remembering the information, including editing, reviewing, reciting, and studying notes. Note making is most effective when it is done soon after notes have been taken, preferably within 24 hours.

Editing steps include:

* Check to be sure that all the main ideas are listed and clearly stated in the left column.

* Check to be sure that all key details are in the right column. If there is irrelevant information, cross it out.

* Ask the teacher or another student to provide any missing information.

* If necessary, reduce wording into more concise phrases.

* Expand abbreviations and wording if notes are unclear.

* Add visual markers (for example: horizontal lines, arrows or numbers) to further organize notes.

* Make sure all note pages are dated and in order.

A reproducible copy of this list is included at the end of this book.

As previously noted, the two-column note format is helpful for reviewing and reciting notes. Students can review and then cover the right column of notes (details), using the main ideas in the left column to help recite and memorize those details. Similarly, the left column (main ideas) can be reviewed and then covered to use the details in the right to help recite and memorize the main ideas.

To reinforce learning for long-term memory, note study should also include some form of writing, such as answering questions or developing summaries. Activities 3 and 4 of *The Key Comprehension Routine* can be combined with two-column note taking to aid in studying.

Other Uses for Two-Column Notes

Notes taken in middle and high school are mostly from expository text or lectures, but the two-column format is also useful for other purposes.

The Two-Column Format to Study Vocabulary

The two-column format can be used for learning new vocabulary. The words are listed in the left column. Definitions, synonyms, and sample sentences containing the words are listed in the right column. Students can fold back or cover either side of the page to study and self-quiz the new vocabulary. Figure E is an example of two-column notes for vocabulary.

Figure E

lexicon	**Definition:** *a language user's knowledge of words*
	Part of speech: *noun*
	Synonym: *dictionary, glossary*
	Antonym: *NA*
	Category/related words: *vocabulary, words, definition, meaning*
	Example: *The words I use to speak.*
	Nonexample: *NA*
	Multiple meanings: *inventory or record*
	Sentence: *Because the boy read every night, he developed a large lexicon and knew more words than most of his friends.*
	Illustration:

migrate	**Definition:** *to move from one country or area and settle in another*
	Part of speech: *verb*
	Synonym: *move*
	Antonym: *stay*
	Category/related words: *travel, movement, different places, relocate, immigrants, settlers, pilgrimage*
	Example: *The Pilgrims migrated to the New World.*
	Nonexample: *The man stayed in the same house his whole life.*
	Multiple meanings: *migration – passage of a group of animals such as birds from one region to another for breeding or feeding*
	Sentence: *The migration of many settlers from the East by covered wagon helped populate the West.*
	Illustration: 

nautical	**Definition:** *related to shipping or navigation of a body of water* **Part of speech:** *adjective* **Synonym:** *maritime, naval* **Antonym:** *land* **Category/related words:** *marine, ocean, boat, sailor* **Example:** *Sails on a boat.* **Nonexample:** *car, train* **Multiple meanings:** *NA* **Sentence:** *The museum had a collection of nautical items that included ship parts and items used by sailors to navigate while crossing the ocean.* **Illustration:**

Narrative Text

Notes from narrative text can be structured to illustrate literary components, such as characters, setting, and theme. The two-column format is helpful for taking notes for any of these components. Figure F illustrates two examples of notes about characters. These characters are from the novel *Johnny Tremain* by Esther Forbes (1943). Figure G demonstrates the use of two-column notes to add details that support parts of a theme. *Hatchet* by Gary Paulson (1987) tells the story of Brian, the sole survivor of a plane crash in the Canadian wilderness. Details from the story describe two types of survival: physical and emotional. As the reader discovers examples from the reading that support each type of survival, these examples can be added to the notes in the right column.

Figure F

Characters from Johnny Tremain	
British army	- General Gage - Colonel Smith - Major Pitcairn - Lieutenant Stranger
Whigs (Patriots)	- John Hancock - Dr. Warren - James Otis - Josiah Quincy
Tories	- Mr. Lyte - Miss Lavinia

Johnny Tremain

Physical description	- skinny - fair, lank hair - 14 years old - thin face - scarred hand
Character description	- hard working - doesn't give up - proud - can keep a secret

Figure G

Theme: Brian's Survival

Physical survival	- found berries to eat - built a shelter with branches against a carved rock - used his hatchet and stone to create a fire spark - found turtle eggs to eat - learned to catch fish
Emotional survival	- thought of his teacher who always told him to stay positive - learned that feeling sorry for yourself doesn't help - tried to keep busy to avoid being depressed - found hope in himself - learned to be more patient

---

Answering Questions

The two-column format also works well for answering comprehension questions. Questions from various levels of Bloom's Taxonomy are listed in the left column, and answers are written in the right. Figure H lists the main ideas from the left column of notes from Figure C on page 72 as questions. Using notes as a basis for generating questions is discussed in greater detail in Activity 4, *Question Generation*.

Figure H

The Red Scare Begins	
Describe three reasons why Americans became more disturbed about the spread of communism in Europe.	
Where did the term Red Scare come from?	
Provide two examples of terrorist acts.	
Why do you think the bombing of Wall Street led people to believe thatcommunists wanted to destroy the government?	
Do you think Palmer's raids were justified? Why or why not?	

Doing Research

Two-column notes can be used to collect information for a research project or report. In order to do so, the student selects targeted information from reading to include in notes. This is a difficult task, because students must sort through a large body of information – often from more than one source – and select specific information that is germane to the research topic. Students can begin to learn this skill as early as 3rd or 4th grade, but instruction must continue through high school. Students will need significant practice using a variety of reading material from different content areas to develop this skill.

Using two-column notes for research can range in difficulty from selecting a few details from a short encyclopedia entry to combining pages of notes from several books and journal articles. Teachers should introduce selective note taking by having students pull one or two main ideas with a few details from a single source and gradually increase the amount of information and number of sources as students become more independent note takers.

Taking Notes from Lectures

Once students are able to take adequate notes from reading, they are ready to practice taking notes from lectures. Many teachers assume that taking notes from lecture is a skill to be taught at the high school or college level. However, it is far more difficult to learn a skill at the same time that you are expected to use it. When note taking from lecture is modeled and practiced in the earlier grades, students can gradually develop this skill and begin to use it in high school.

The *I, We, You* gradual release of responsibility model described in Chapter 1 is particularly useful for teaching notes from lectures. Using this model, the teacher initially demonstrates taking notes and stops at various points to think aloud and explain why she is writing certain words and phrases in the left or right column. Guided practice should follow: the whole class can generate notes while the teacher writes them on the board. At this time, it is helpful to pose meta-cognitive questions like "How many details did I just give to support my point?" or "What was the main theme of the lecture?" Students can also gather in small groups after a lecture to compare their notes and have meta-cognitive discussions about essential information that should be in the notes. This also allows students to hear alternative ways of paraphrasing the information.

Note taking can be broken down into structured steps to be completed one at a time. For example, teachers can initially provide a set of notes with all the main ideas and a few details. At first, students listen and add the remaining details to the notes. With practice, note taking becomes more automatic; gradually, students can take a full set of notes independently.

Another way to scaffold note taking is to start with short, scripted oral presentations of information about a topic with which the students are familiar (about a paragraph's worth of information). Provide time for the students to complete and edit their notes before moving on to the next segment of information. Gradually increase the length of the oral presentation as students become more adept at listening and taking notes simultaneously.

Yet another way to scaffold is to repeat oral presentations. The first time information is presented, the students listen only to get a sense of the topic and some of the details. The second time, students take only main idea notes in the left column. During the third presentation, they add details in the right column.

Recognizing Speaker Cues

Speakers often provide verbal or body language cues that can help note takers identify key information from a lecture. Students benefit from direct instruction in how to recognize these cues. Teachers should take a moment during lectures to point out some of these cues (Sedita, 2002), including:

* A speaker usually pauses before moving on to a new main idea.
* Important information is often repeated or emphasized, and it should be included in notes.
* Transition words and phrases like "next," "finally," and "the most important" signal key information or an organizational pattern that the speaker may be using (e.g., listing, comparing and contrasting, or describing).
* A speaker provides organization cues through body language: shifting weight, looking back at notes, pointing, looking more directly at the audience.
* Changes in volume, pace, or inflection of the speaker's voice may indicate a change in the main idea or emphasize important details.
* Introductory and concluding remarks often provide a review of the main ideas in the presentation.

Activity 1: Generating Notes

Part 1

Directions: *Using classroom reading material or content from a unit of study you will teach, generate a set of two-column notes. You can use the template below or a separate piece of paper.*

Part 2

Directions: Turn the main ideas from the left side of your notes into questions that students can use the details to answer. Add the questions in the left column of your notes.

Part 3

Directions: Develop or describe an activity you could use to scaffold these notes for struggling students.

_____

_____

_____

_____

_____

_____

_____

_____

_____

_____

_____

_____

_____

_____

_____

_____

_____

_____

_____

_____

_____

_____

Activity 3
Summary

A summary is an overview of the most important information from a reading selection, class lesson, or lecture. To summarize, one must integrate ideas and generalize from the text information. Writing a summary helps students see the big picture and process the information more deeply as they use their own words to generate the summary. Summarizing requires students to monitor their comprehension and thoroughly understand the material they are reading before they can reduce it to a few words. If they cannot summarize, then it is clear that they do not understand the information. Research has shown that summarizing is one of the most effective strategies for improving comprehension and writing (National Reading Panel, 2000; Snow, 2002; Graham & Perin, 2007).

A summary reduces a large quantity of information to the most important main ideas. It is a shorter, condensed version of the original material, and it does not contain many details. Anderson and Hidi (1988-1989) describe summarizing as a selection and reduction process. First, students must decide and select which information is important; they must then condense that information by substituting general ideas for more detailed ones.

The squeezing of a sponge provides a good metaphor for the summarizing process: The information from which a summary will be generated is heavy with details, like a sponge that is full of water. The information is then reduced to a series of main idea phrases, like a sponge being squeezed to remove the water. To write the full summary, the main ideas are then expanded into sentences, just as a sponge expands somewhat after it is let go. The summary is a complete overview of the original, without all of the details.

Summaries can be developed from both narrative and expository text. The most common summary from narrative text is a plot summary, which is constructed by identifying and condensing the most important events in a story. Summaries from expository text are generated from the main ideas. A summary can also be generated from non-text sources such as a lecture, class discussion, video, or event (e.g., a soccer game). In all cases, the student must first identify the important events or main ideas in order to develop a summary.

Limited and Big Picture Summaries

Summaries can vary in length and scope. A limited summary can be generated from a short reading passage, such as a newspaper article, or several paragraphs from a book. Typically, limited summaries are derived from a few paragraph main ideas. Below is an example of a limited summary generated from a later section of this chapter entitled *Writing Skills* (see page 97):

Summarizing is a writing task often confused with other types of writing. It is best used as a comprehension strategy. However, it does require knowledge of basic writing skills common to all types of writing. If a student cannot generate a summary, the teacher should determine if it is because of a lack of understanding or a lack of writing skills.

On the other hand, a big picture summary may be more appropriate for summarizing a longer reading selection such as a textbook chapter or a short story. Big picture summaries tend to be longer and may even consist of several paragraphs. Below is an example of a big picture summary generated from this entire chapter:

A summary is an overview of the most important information and supports comprehension. Writing a summary entails reducing a large quantity of information to a condensed version of the original material. Summaries can be generated from narrative or expository text; however, they can also be generated from non-text sources such as a lecture or a video. A limited summary is used for summarizing a short amount of information, and a big picture summary is used to summarizing a larger amount of information such as a book chapter.

There are several steps to generating a summary. First, the student must identify the main ideas. Next, the student will develop the ideas into sentences and include transition words to make connections between the sentences. Finally, the summary should be proofed for content, spelling and punctuation. For the first step of identifying main ideas, there are several scaffolding tools that can be used: a summary template, a topic web, or a set of two-column notes.

Summarizing is a writing task often confused with other types of writing. It is best used as a comprehension strategy. However, it does require knowledge of basic writing skills common to all types of writing. The use of transition words is an example of a basic writing skill that can improve summary writing.

How to Write a Summary

The first step is to read to identify the main ideas. The main ideas must then be condensed and paraphrased. If the reading is short, there may only be a few main ideas; for lengthier reading selections, there may be a hierarchy of section main ideas, sub-section main ideas, and paragraph main ideas.

After the main ideas have been identified, the student should begin the summary with an introductory statement. Next, each of the main ideas must be developed into sentences. Depending on the amount of information to be summarized, these sentences may generate either a single- or multi-paragraph summary. Transition words should then be added to connect the sentences and paragraphs. Finally, students should proofread the summary to be sure all the important main ideas were included and sufficiently explained, as well as to edit spelling or punctuation errors. Figure A reviews the steps for writing a summary. A reproducible copy of this list is provided at the end of this book.

Figure A

How To Write A Summary

1. Read the material and identify the main ideas. Distinguish the main ideas from the details.

2. Write the main ideas in phrase form.

3. Begin the summary with an introductory statement.

4. Turn the main ideas into sentences, occasionally including details when necessary to convey the main idea.

5. Combine the sentences into one or more paragraphs.

6. Use transition words to connect the sentences and the paragraphs.

7. Proofread the summary for punctuation, spelling, sentence structure, and content.

Teachers should explicitly teach the following guidelines for writing a summary:

* The first sentence of the summary should be a general statement that introduces the overall topic of the summary.

* Although the summary should be developed primarily from main ideas, it may be necessary to incorporate some details to adequately convey a main idea.

* Each main idea does not necessarily need its own sentence. Two related main ideas can be combined into one sentence, and more than one sentence may be required to render a single main idea.

* Once they are taken out of the text, the order of main ideas is flexible.

* A summary depends on the length of the material being summarized; it can be a single paragraph or several.

Blueprints for Summarizing

Summarizing is a difficult skill to teach and to use. One reason for this is that the student must apply several sets of skills in order to generate a summary:

* **Comprehension Skills.** The student must understand what he is reading, identify the main ideas, and state them in his own words.

* **Organizational Skills.** The student must remember the main ideas and then organize and combine them into sentences.

✳ **Writing Skills.** The student must apply paraphrasing skills to describe the main ideas in his own words, as well as apply general writing skills.

When teaching summarizing, the eventual goal is for students to independently follow the steps for generating a summary and apply the comprehension, organization, and writing skills noted above. Until students reach this point, there are three tools that will help scaffold the task of summarizing. We consider these tools "blueprints" for writing a summary, because they are like a plan or framework for building a summary.

First, a summary template can be used to remind students of each step in the process. Figure B is the summary template used in *The Key Comprehension Routine*. A reproducible copy of this template is available at the end of this book. Figure C is a student example of the template's use in writing a summary of a chapter from *The Lord of the Flies* by William Golding (1954).

Figure B

Summary Template

1. List the main ideas in phrase form.

   - _____
   - _____
   - _____
   - _____
   - _____
   - _____
   - _____

2. Write an introductory sentence that states the topic of the summary.

   _____
   _____
   _____

3. Turn the main ideas into sentences using your own words. You can combine some of the main ideas into one sentence.

   _____
   _____
   _____
   _____
   _____
   _____
   _____
   _____
   _____
   _____
   _____

4. Add transition words from the list below or from the transition poster.
   first, next, finally, before, after, during, later, also, another, in addition, in conclusion, to sum up, similarly, however, on the contrary, most important, for example, as a result, therefore

5. Proofread and edit your summary.

Figure C

> Edwin
>
> ## Summary Template
> Lord of the flies (Chpt 4)
>
> 1. List the main ideas in phrase form.
>   - 1. Theres Panic on island
>   - 2. Ship Sails by them.
>   - 3. Fire goes out.
>   - 4. They Kill the Pig.
>   - _____
>   - _____
>   - _____
>
> 2. Write an introductory sentence that states the topic of the summary.
>   There is alot of Panic and arguing on the island.
>
> 3. Turn the main ideas into sentences using your own words. You can combine some of the main ideas into one sentence.
>   - 1.) Ralph see's ship Sails by them and wonders why they did'it stop.
>   - 2.) The reason why they did'it stop was because fire was out.
>   - 3.) They are lacking food so they decide to kill a pig.
>
> 4. Add transition words from the list below or from the transition poster.
>   *first, next, finally, before, after, during, later, also, another, in addition, in conclusion, to sum up, similarly, however, on the contrary, most important, for example, as a result, therefore*
>
> 5. Proofread and edit your summary.

In addition to the summary template, top-down topic webs and two-column notes can also be helpful blueprints for developing a summary. Because a top-down topic web contains just topics and sub-topics, all of the information from a web should (usually) be included in the summary. Because two-column notes contain a lot of detail in the right column, all of the information from the left column should (usually) be included in the summary – but not many details from the right column. Figure D illustrates how a summary is generated from a topic web. Because this web covers information from a section of a science textbook that is several pages long, it is an example of a big picture summary.

Figure D

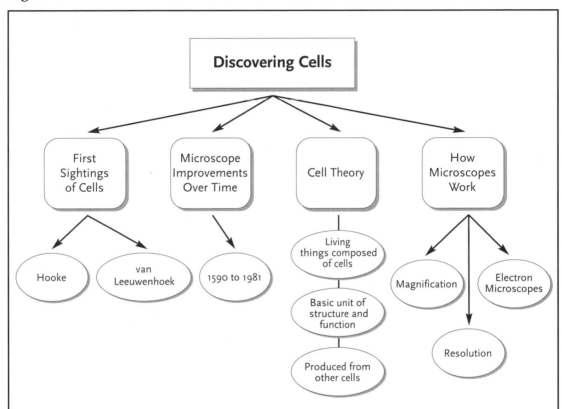

Cells were first discovered by Hooke and van Leeuwenhoek after the microscope was invented. Between 1590 and 1981, many improvements were made to microscopes. Once cells were found in all living things, the creation of cell theory confirmed that all living things are composed of cells. Also, cells are the basic unit of structure and function in living things. Finally, cells are produced from other cells. Microscopes let us see cells because of magnification and resolution. The newest microscopes use electrons instead of light.

Figure E is an example of a summary that was generated from the two-column notes on page 72 from *The Red Scare Begins*. Because the notes are from a shorter reading selection, it is an example of a limited summary. The main ideas in the left column provide the basis of the summary, which includes just a few of the details from the right column.

Figure E

Americans disturbed about spread of communism in Europe	- Bolsheviks win in Russian Revolution - communist sympathizers in U.S. - labor problems turning radical
Suspicion of communists	- Americans suspicious since WWI - known as the Red Scare
Terrorism in America	- Mayor Hanson of Seattle breaks up strike then receives mail bomb - Senator Hartwick receives mail bomb - bomb destroys Attorney General Palmer's home - 30 mail bombs discovered
Wall Street bomb blamed on communists	- high point of tension - 30 people killed
Palmer's raids on suspected communists	- law enforcement raids on suspected communists Over 6000 arrested, 550 deported Even government officials lost civil liberties

Summary, The Red Scare Begins

The Red Scare began after World War I. Americans were worried about communism spreading in Europe. <u>As a result</u>, many Americans became suspicious of communists. This was known as the Red Scare. Several terrorist acts occurred, including a bombing of Wall Street, which was blamed on communists. Under Attorney General Palmer, law enforcement arrested and deported many suspected communists. <u>In addition</u>, many people lost their civil liberties.

Figure F provides another example of a big picture summary generated from a topic web. The web was developed from a full chapter of a social studies textbook. The topics, represented in circles, and the subtopics, represented in rectangles, were combined into sentences to create the summary.

Figure F

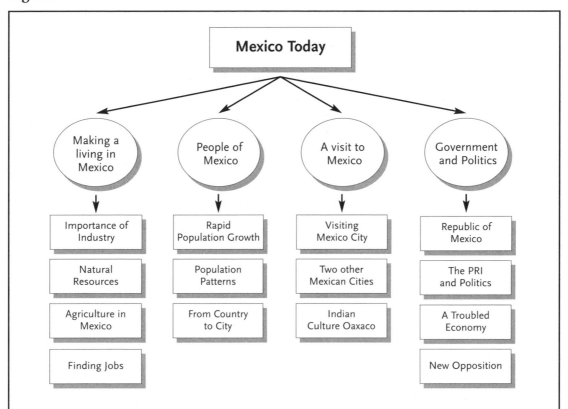

Mexicans make a living by working in industry, tourism, agriculture, or mining minerals and oil. <u>However</u>, it is hard for many Mexicans to find work. The population of Mexico has grown a lot. Most of the people live in the middle of the country. <u>Over the years</u>, many Mexicans have moved from the countryside to the cities to find work and go to school. Mexico City is the national capital. It has a long history. <u>Therefore</u>, there are many interesting sites to see. <u>Another</u> city, Oaxaca, has a lot of Indian culture sites. Mexico is a republic with an elected president and representatives from many states. The Institutional Revolutionary Party is the oldest and strongest political party in Mexico. <u>However</u>, a poor economy has pushed many Mexicans to support a new party called the National Action Party.

Figure G provides another example of a limited summary generated from two-column notes. As you can see, these notes list three main ideas in the left column taken from three paragraphs in the textbook chapter from above, *Mexico Today,* and the details in the right column are taken from the sentences in those paragraphs. Again, the main ideas in the left column are the basis of the summary, which includes just a few of the details from the right column.

Figure G

The Importance of Industry

1. Mexico is one of most industrialized countries in Latin America	• . Factories make many things: iron, steel, glass, chemicals, paper, cement, textiles, electrical equip, processed foods • Auto manufacturing is major industry • Manufacturing means making of goods on large scale, especially by machines
2. Manufacturing covers big area	• Stretches from Veracruz on east coast • To Guadalajara near western side • Mexico City, Puebla, Cuernavaca, Toluca, & Leon are in manufacturing area
3. Tourism is big business	• 10% of GNP came from tourism • GNP is total value of nations' goods & services produced in 1 year • To attract tourists: weather & scenery, hotel/restaurant ads, tourist agencies, efficient transportation

Importance of Industry

Mexico is one of the most industrialized countries of Latin America. Mexico manufactures many things in its factories, including automobiles. The factories can be found all over the country. <u>Another</u> major business in Mexico is tourism. Tourism is strong because of the good weather and scenery. <u>In addition</u>, Mexico promotes tourism.

Writing Skills

It is important to note that summarizing is a very specific kind of writing task. Students and teachers often confuse summarizing with other types of writing, such as:

* Written response to test or open response questions

* Five-paragraph essay

* Journal entry

* Authentic or creative writing

* Descriptive or persuasive writing

* Research or report writing

First and foremost, summarizing is a comprehension strategy and a tool for demonstrating the student's understanding of big ideas from content information.

There are several basic writing skills common to all types of writing required to generate a quality summary, including:

* Ability to vary word choice, to generate synonyms, and to use appropriate transition words

* Ability to combine sentences, create compound and complex sentences, change word order within a sentence, and apply appropriate grammatical rules

* Ability to develop introductory and concluding sentences, reorder sentences, and create new paragraphs when sub-topics change

* Ability to proofread for spelling, capitalization and punctuation, and content

Teachers must distinguish between a student who cannot comprehend the main ideas and a student who is having difficulty writing about them. Struggling writers may recognize the main ideas and simply need help with the semantic, syntactic, or editing skills needed to write the summary.

Transition Words

Transition words (e.g., before, likewise, eventually) are useful for connecting sentences in a summary. Struggling readers often are not adept at using transition words, or at using them correctly. They may require examples and guided practice to develop this skill. It is helpful to post a list of transition words in the classroom and to have students keep a copy of the same list in their notebooks for reference when writing. Figure H contains a list of common transition words. A reproducible copy of this list is available at the end of this book.

Figure H

Transition Words and Phrases	
To indicate a time relationship	after, afterward, after that, at first, at this time, before, beginning with, beyond, during, earlier, ending with, eventually, finally, following, from then on, in the meantime, last, later, meanwhile, next, now, since, soon, then, until, while
To indicate spatial placement	below, beside, between, beyond, farther on, here, next to, parallel with
To list or present a series of ideas	after, after that, finally, first, lastly, next, second, third
To add information or continue a line of thought	also, another, besides, further, furthermore, in addition, likewise, moreover, similarly
To summarize or show conclusion	accordingly, finally, in conclusion, in other words, in short, to conclude, to sum up, to summarize
To show comparison	by comparison, compared to, in like manner, likewise, similarly
To show contrast	although, but, however, in contrast, nevertheless, on the contrary, on the other hand, unlike
To repeat information or stress a point	above all, in fact, in other words, most important, once again, to repeat
To provide an example or illustrate a point	for example, for instance, such as, to illustrate, that is
To show cause and effect	as a result, because, because of, caused by, consequently, for that reason, that is why, therefore, thus
To state the obvious	certainly, granted that, in fact, most certainly, naturally, obviously, of course, surely, undoubtedly, without a doubt

Activity 1: Generating a Summary

Part 1
<u>Directions</u>: *Use the summary template to generate a summary from a sample of your classroom reading material. Write the completed summary below.*

_____

_____

_____

_____

_____

_____

_____

_____

_____

_____

Part 2
<u>Directions</u>: *Use the top-down topic web or two-column notes you generated in the earlier chapters in this book to generate a summary.*

_____

_____

_____

_____

_____

_____

_____

_____

_____

_____

Activity 4
Question Generation

Question generation can be used as a before, during, and after activity for reading or read aloud. Generating questions before reading helps students make predictions about what they will learn and focus on the most important information. It also helps students read (or listen) with greater purpose because they are searching for the answers to their questions. Question generation during reading encourages students to be more thoughtful and to monitor their comprehension. After reading, question generation encourages students to review and think critically about what they read and to express that information in their own words to answer the questions. It is important to note that the goal of question generation is to teach students to generate their own questions.

Rosenshine, Meister, and Chapman (1996) were among the first to review studies about students taught to generate questions as a comprehension strategy, and their findings indicated that teaching the strategy results in comprehension gains. There is also significant evidence that learning to generate and answer questions while reading improves memory, integration and identification of main ideas, as well as overall comprehension (National Reading Panel, 2000; Trabasso & Bouchard, 2002).

Active Learning Through Questioning

Instruction in question generation and answering helps students get more out of reading by finding and using information in the text to answer questions. It also helps students learn to ask themselves questions about what they read and to actively process information in text to answer those questions. By generating questions, "students become aware of whether they can answer the questions, and thus whether they understand what they are reading" (Lehr, 2005, p. 19).

In order to generate questions, students must first identify which information is important enough to use as the basis for a question. As they attempt to answer their questions, they must determine whether they have in fact comprehended what they have read or heard in a read aloud. Generating questions does not come naturally to many students, especially in the primary grades. They tend to generate simple *who, what, where,* and *when* questions that require factual information to answer. It is much more difficult to generate complex questions that require critical thinking, but it is important to teach students how to create the kinds of questions that require them to go beyond readily available information. A combination of both sorts of questions is necessary. Some should require students to learn supporting detail information, and others should require them to infer or apply new information from text.

Teachers should provide direct instruction, modeling, and significant guided practice for question generation. Specifically:

* Provide samples of various question types and guided practice for generating questions.
* Teach the meaning and use of key question terms.
* Teach a continuum of questions (i.e., Bloom's Taxonomy), ranging from simple, fact-based questions to complex, critical thinking questions.

The Key Comprehension Routine Questioning Model: Bloom's Taxonomy

Students should be taught and encouraged to generate questions at different levels. *The Key Comprehension Routine* uses a continuum for question generation based on Bloom's Taxonomy (Bloom, 1956) because it incorporates multiple levels of thinking, from simple, factual knowledge to various kinds of critical thinking. Six levels comprise the revised Bloom's Taxonomy (Anderson and Krathwhohl, 2001): Remembering, Understanding, Applying, Analyzing, Evaluating, and Creating. See Figure A.

Figure A

Bloom's Revised Taxonomy		
Remembering	recalling information (facts)	recognizing, listing, identifying, retrieving, naming, finding
Understanding	explaining ideas or concepts (in your own words)	interpreting, summarizing, paraphrasing, describing, explaining
Applying	using information in another familiar situation (life and use)	implementing, carrying out, executing
Analyzing	breaking information into parts to explore understandings and relationships (compare/contrast)	comparing, organizing, deconstructing, distinguishing, arranging
Evaluating	justifying a decision or course of action (fair/unfair, right/wrong, ranking)	debating, hypothesizing, critiquing, appraising, judging
Creating	generating new ideas, products, or ways of viewing things (what if?)	designing, constructing, planning, producing, inventing

In order to develop critical thinking skills, students should be taught to generate and answer questions at every level of Bloom's Taxonomy. Questions at the lower levels are important for learning basic factual information, while questions at the higher levels engage students and require them to apply critical thinking skills like critiquing and making inferences.

Figure B lists sample questions from all levels of Bloom's Taxonomy for the story *Hatchet* and for a math lesson. Additional classroom examples of question generation from various subject areas are also available at the end of this book.

Figure B

<table>
<tr><td colspan="2" align="center">From *Hatchet* by Gary Paulson (1987):</td></tr>
<tr><td>**Remembering:**</td><td>What gift did Brian receive from his mother?</td></tr>
<tr><td>**Understanding:**</td><td>Describe what happened when the plane crashed.</td></tr>
<tr><td>**Applying:**</td><td>Have you ever been lost in the woods (or lost someplace else)? Share your experience with your collaborative group.</td></tr>
<tr><td>**Analyzing:**</td><td>Compare/contrast Brian with Karana in *Island of the Blue Dolphins*.</td></tr>
<tr><td>**Evaluating:**</td><td>Should Brian have told his father "the secret?" Justify your answer.</td></tr>
<tr><td>**Creating:**</td><td>Create an alternate ending to the book.</td></tr>
</table>

<table>
<tr><td colspan="2" align="center">From a math lesson about *slope:*</td></tr>
<tr><td>**Remembering:**</td><td>Identify the four kinds of slope.</td></tr>
<tr><td>**Understanding:**</td><td>Explain what a negative slope looks like.</td></tr>
<tr><td>**Applying:**</td><td>Illustrate positive slope in a real-life situation.</td></tr>
<tr><td>**Analyzing:**</td><td>Distinguish between the equations of vertical and horizontal slope.</td></tr>
<tr><td>**Evaluating:**</td><td>Rank the given six slopes in order of lowest to greatest force required to move a given object.</td></tr>
<tr><td>**Creating:**</td><td>Design a proposal for a ski/snowboarding resort identifying the slope at which skiing or snowboarding becomes dangerous. Design the proposal such that the resort will be enticed to hire your design company.</td></tr>
</table>

Question Terminology

Many students are not able to effectively answer questions, especially on standardized tests, because they are not familiar with many question words and/or do not know their meaning. Similarly, students cannot generate different types of questions because their repertoire of question words is limited. Teachers should both provide a list of question words and model their use in generating questions. Figure C provides a list of question terms organized along Bloom's Taxonomy. A reproducible copy of this list is included at the end of this book. Note that some question words can be used to generate questions at more than one level; therefore, it is important for students to focus on the kind and level of question, rather than simply choosing a word at random from the list.

Figure C

Remembering	Understanding	Applying	Analyzing	Evaluating	Creating
Cite	Describe	Adapt	Analyze	Appraise	Assemble
Define	Discuss	Apply	Arrange	Assess	Compile
Find	Explain	Compute	Categorize	Choose	Compose
Give an	Interpret	Demonstrate	Compare	Conclude	Concoct
example	Paraphrase	Dramatize	Contrast	Criticize	Construct
Identify	Report	Draw	Deconstruct	Critique	Create
Label	Restate in	Illustrate	Detect	Debate	Design
List	own words	Implement	Dissect	Deduce	Develop
Locate	Retell	Interview	Distinguish	Defend	Devise
Match	Review	Make	Examine	Hypothesize	Formulate
Name	Summarize	Operate	Group	Judge	Generate
Quote	Translate	Practice	Inspect	Justify	Imagine
Recall		Role play	Integrate	Prioritize	Invent
Recite		Sequence	Organize	Rank	Make
Recognize		Solve	Probe	Rate	Originate
Retrieve		Use	Research	Reject	Prepare
Show			Separate	Validate	Produce
			Sift		Set up
					What if?

Figure D provides a list of question prompts that can be used to generate questions at all levels of Bloom's Taxonomy. A reproducible copy of this list is included at the end of this book.

Figure D

Level	Prompts
Remembering	Where is... What did... Who was... When did... How many... Locate it in the story... Point to the...
Understanding	Tell me in your own words... What does it mean... Give me an example of... Describe what... Make a map of... What is the main idea of...
Applying	What would happen to you if... Would you have done the same as... If you were there, would you... How would you solve the problem... In the library, find information about...
Analyzing	What things would you have used... What other ways could... What things are similar/different? What things couldn't have happened in real life? What kind of person is... What caused _____ to act the way she/he did?
Evaluating	Would you recommend this book? Why? Why not? Select the best...Why is it the best? What do you think will happen to... Why do you think that? Rank the events in order of importance. Which character would you most like to meet? Why? Was _____ good or bad? Why? Did you like the story? Why?
Creating	What would it be like if... What would it be like to live... Design a... Pretend you are a... What would have happened if... Why/why not? Use your imagination to draw a picture of... Add a new item on your own... Tell/write a different ending...

Adapted from: Fisher, D.B., and Frey, N. (2007). "Checking for Understanding." Alexandria, VA: ASCD.

Introducing and Scaffolding Question Generation

It may take a while for students to become familiar with question terminology and automatically generate questions at all six levels of Bloom's Taxonomy. Teachers play an important role in leading students through explicit instruction and thinking aloud to model question generation.

The Key Comprehension Routine recommends the following scope and sequence for introducing and practicing question generation:

 ✳ Teach one or two levels of questions at a time, starting with *Remembering* and *Understanding*. Gradually introduce higher levels.

 ✳ Provide examples of questions about a familiar topic from everyday life, and label the level.

 ✳ Provide examples of questions about a familiar topic from everyday life, and have students label the level.

 ✳ Teach question word vocabulary, starting with 1-2 of the simplest terms. Gradually introduce additional terms.

 ✳ Have students work in small groups to generate questions about everyday topics at all levels.

 ✳ Provide examples of questions about reading passages and classroom content information.

 ✳ Have students work in small groups to generate questions about reading passages and classroom content information.

Students should be given the opportunity to work with peers to generate questions collaboratively. As students discuss information, consider different levels of thinking, and choose which question terms to incorporate, this cooperation enables a richer thinking and language experience.

Scaffolding

As with the other *Key Comprehension Routine* strategies, a good way to scaffold instruction is for students to generate questions using familiar, everyday information. Because they are already familiar with the information, they can turn their attention to the question level, appropriate question terms, and the level of thinking required to answer the question. For example, Figure E lists questions generated about a restaurant menu and a school basketball game.

Figure E

Example 1: Questions about a restaurant menu

Question Level	*Question*
Remembering	List three options for appetizers.
Understanding	Describe the courses available at this restaurant.
Applying	Use the menu to order a three-course meal.
Analyzing	Which menu items are suitable for a vegetarian?
Evaluating	Rank the three desserts from best to worst. Explain your ranking.
Creating	Create a new menu with the same ingredients used in the items on this menu.

Example 2: Questions about a school basketball game

Question Level	*Question*
Remembering	Name the team captains.
Understanding	Explain the rules of the game.
Applying	Illustrate three important plays from the game.
Analyzing	Compare and contrast the offense and defense of each team.
Evaluating	Which team played better? Justify your answer.
Creating	What if each team lost its best player? Imagine how the game might have ended.

Activity 1: Generate Your Own Questions

Directions: Choose an everyday topic and generate questions at each level of Bloom's Taxonomy.

Question Level	Question
Remembering	
Understanding	
Applying	
Analyzing	
Evaluating	
Creating	

Another way to scaffold instruction is to provide the questions and ask students to identify the level of each. Students can do this individually or work in small groups.

Activity 2: What Level?

Directions: Review the questions below about *The Key Comprehension Routine*. Label the type of each question.

Question Level	Question
	Draw a top-down topic web that illustrates the four activities in *The Key Comprehension Routine*.
	Describe *The Key Comprehension Routine*.
	Create a lesson plan that incorporates a top-down topic web, two-column notes, and question generation.
	Do you think using *The Key Comprehension Routine* with your students will improve their comprehension? Why?
	List the six levels of Bloom's Taxonomy.
	Compare and contrast outlining with two-column notes.

Use Visuals and Manipulatives

The use of manipulatives can help enforce the notion of a continuum of questions. It can also help students recognize distinctions among the levels of thinking and associated terms and question words for each level. Examples include:

* **Posters or bulletin boards.** Create a chart that illustrates Bloom's taxonomy on poster paper or a classroom bulletin board. See Figure F, a chart with cue words for each level arranged along the steps of a ladder. A copy of this chart is provided in the reproducibles at the end of the book. Figure G is another helpful visual: As a mountain climber ascends the mountain, he climbs to higher levels of thinking.

* **Buckets or containers.** Use six containers to represent the levels of Bloom's taxonomy. Label each container with the name of a level. For more support, add a description about the level on the label. Here are two suggestions for using the containers:

  * Organize students in pairs or small groups. Write questions on index cards, and give each group a set of questions that includes at least one question from each level of Bloom's Taxonomy. Place the six containers at the front of the room. Ask the groups to identify the level of each question in their sets and place them in the appropriate buckets at the front of the room.

  * Organize students into six groups. Give each group a container labeled with a level of Bloom's Taxonomy (e.g., one group will have *Remembering,* another will have *Understanding,* etc.). Ask the groups to generate at least one question at the level of thinking on their container, write the question on an index card, and place the card in the bucket. Next, rotate the containers so each group has a new question level. Continue the activity until all containers have been passed to all groups at least once.

* **Cards or craft sticks with question words or prompts:** Using large colored craft sticks or colored note cards (you will need six different colors), assign a color to each level of Bloom's Taxonomy. Assemble the sticks or cards in groups of the same color. Write each of the prompts and/or question terms (see Figures C and D) on a stick or card. Then place them in a container labeled with the level to which they correspond. Follow the steps for the second activity in the bullet above, but ask students to pick a stick or card and use the word(s) or prompt on it in their question.

Figure F

Bloom's Taxonomy

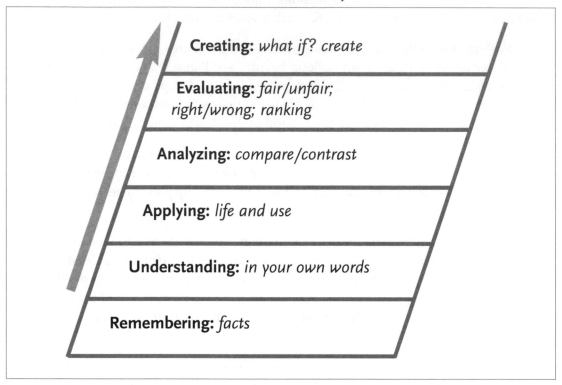

Creating: *what if? create*

Evaluating: *fair/unfair; right/wrong; ranking*

Analyzing: *compare/contrast*

Applying: *life and use*

Understanding: *in your own words*

Remembering: *facts*

Figure G

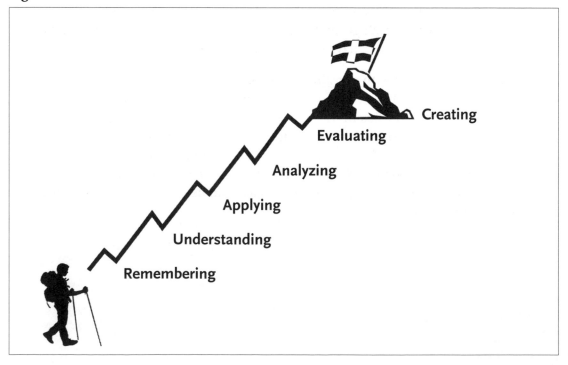

Creating

Evaluating

Analyzing

Applying

Understanding

Remembering

Note that once students have generated their own questions about information they are learning from reading or classroom instruction, the teacher can draw from these questions to generate a quiz or test. This introduces students to the idea that part of studying as they move into upper grades includes determining possible test questions.

Topics for Questions

Questions at all levels of thinking can be generated from any topic. Students can use three sources to identify topics for question generation:

 ✳ Chapter titles, headings, and sub-headings

 ✳ Top-down topic webs

 ✳ Two-column notes

Activity 3: Question Generation from Web & Notes

Directions: Using a top-down topic web, the set of two-column notes that you generated during training, or headings from your classroom textbook, generate questions at every level of Bloom's Taxonomy.

Question Level	Question
Remembering	
Understanding	
Applying	
Analyzing	
Evaluating	
Creating	

Using Question Generation to Support Extended Discussion of Text Meaning

As noted in Chapter 4, opportunities for extended discussion of text meaning improve the literacy skills of students in grades 4-12. The goal for reading should not be just to obtain facts or literal meaning from text, but also to make deeper interpretations, generalizations, and conclusions. (Kamil, et al., 2008). Kamil and his colleagues make the following points about questioning as it relates to the discussion of text meaning:

✳ Most successful applications of strategy instruction involved extended opportunities for discussing texts while students are learning to independently apply such strategies as summarizing, making predictions, and generating and answering questions . . . (p. 22)

✳ Questions that lead to good discussion are described as authentic in that they ask a real question that may be open to multiple points of view. (p. 23)

✳ Discussions that have an impact on student reading comprehension feature exchanges between teachers and students or among students, where students are asked to defend their statements either by reasoning or by referring to information in the text. (p. 23)

✳ One form of preparation for text discussion involves selecting and developing questions that can stimulate students to think reflectively about the text and make high-level connections or inferences. (p. 23)

✳ In a sustained discussion initial questions are likely to be followed by other questions that respond to the student's answer and lead to further thinking and elaboration. (p. 23)

Questions about the text generated from the lower levels of Bloom's Taxonomy (remembering, understanding, applying) require a focus on factual information that can then be used to answer questions from the upper levels (analyzing, evaluating, creating).

Other Models for Teaching Question Generation

There are several other effective models for teaching students how to generate and answer questions in order to improve reading comprehension:

✳ **Question/Answer Relationships (QAR)** (Raphael, 1982, 1986). Students are taught to recognize and generate four types of questions – *right there, think and search, author and you,* and *on my own.*

✳ **Reciprocal Teaching** (Palinscar and Brown, 1985). This model includes a questioning component whereby students pose questions based on a portion of a text that a group has read.

✳ **KWL Strategy** (Ogle, 1986, 1989). Students complete a three-column template: *what I know, what I want to know, what I learned.*

✳ **Questioning the Author** (Beck, McKeown, Hamilton and Kucan, 1997). This model teaches students to develop *queries* for the author. The *queries* are designed to make students think more deeply about the text and the author's point of view.

NOTES:

Part IV

Putting it all together

Chapter 5
Combining Activities

As previously noted, instruction is more effective when several strategies are combined rather than used alone; in fact, the National Reading Panel (2000) found that the use of strategies improved results in standardized comprehension tests when used in combination. Strategies enhance instruction even further when used together in a flexible, responsive interaction between the teacher and the students (Gaskins, 1998; Pressley, 2000; Duke et al., 2004). Two instructional models combine activities into a routine and have been successful in improving comprehension:

❋ **Collaborative Strategic Reading** (Klingner et al., 2001): This routine combines four reading comprehension strategies with cooperative learning groups or paired learning. The strategy activities are Preview, Click and Clunk, Get the Gist, and Wrap Up.

❋ **Reciprocal Teaching** (Palinscar & Brown, 1984): This routine provides students with four discrete reading strategies that are actively and consciously used as texts are processed with small-group collaboration, monitored by the teacher. The strategies are Clarifying, Predicting, Questioning, and Summarizing.

Similar to these models, *The Key Comprehension Routine* combines main idea and text structure skills with four activities (Top-Down Topic Webs, Two-Column Notes, Question Generation, Summarizing). The routine also emphasizes using small groups to practice the strategy activities. Any one of the four strategy activities can be used alone, but when two or more are combined students are more likely to understand and remember information they are reading and learning. Figure A illustrates the relationship between *The Key Comprehension Routine*'s four activities.

Figure A

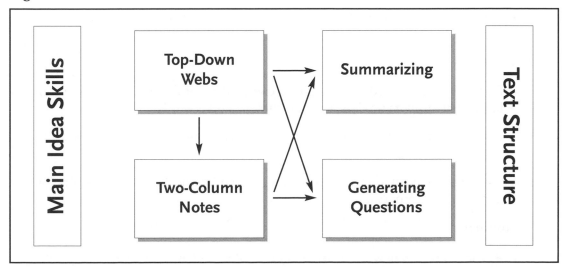

As shown in Figure A, the activities can be combined as follows:

✳ **A top-down topic web can be used to generate a set of two-column notes.** The topics or sub-topics from a web are carried over into the left column of notes and details are added in the right column.

✳ **A top-down topic web can be used to generate a summary.** The topics and sub-topics from the web are used to develop the list of main ideas that are then used to generate a summary.

✳ **A top-down topic web can be used to generate questions.** The topics and sub-topics in the web are converted to questions that can be used before, during or after reading.

✳ **A set of two-column notes can be used to generate a summary.** The main ideas in the left column and a few supporting details from the right column are used to generate the summary.

✳ **A set of two-column notes can be used to generate questions.** Main ideas or details from either column are used to generate questions.

Teaching the Purpose of an Activity

In addition to teaching students how to use a strategy activity, teachers should also explain the purpose for each activity and when it can be used. For example:

✳ **Top-Down Topic Web**

- Provides a visual representation of the big picture.

- Can be used as a before activity to activate background knowledge, make predictions, and provide a road map for how concepts and information are presented.

- Can be used as a during activity to make connections between topics and to avoid getting overwhelmed by details.

- Can be used as an after activity to study, generate questions, or generate a summary.

✳ **Two-Column Notes**

- Provides a condensed and organized compilation of the main ideas and most important supporting details in the student's own words.

- Can be used as a during activity to actively read and listen, and to capture essential information.

- Can be used as an after activity to study, generate questions and answers, or generate a summary.

✳ **Summary**

- Provides an overview of the main ideas in the student's own words.

- Can be used as a during activity to reinforce comprehension.

- Can be used as an after activity to study.

✳ **Question Generation**

- Fosters comprehension at different levels of thinking.

- Can be used as a before activity to activate prior knowledge and generate curiosity.

- Can be used as a during activity to actively search for information to answer the questions.

- Can be used as an after activity to study.

Examples of Combined Activities

The remainder of this chapter presents examples of combined activities applied to several subject areas, including main idea and detail identification in text, top-down webs, two-column notes, question generation, and summaries.

Example 1: English Language Arts – Reading Passage

Figure A: Text Passage (details underlined)

¯27 The Mysterious Iceman

Put yourself in these tourists' position. You are walking an icy mountain path in the Alps in Europe. Suddenly you <u>spot</u> a body on the ground, face downward and stuck to the ice. You think someone may have been murdered or in a fatal accident. So you rush back and call the police. The police, however, quickly realize that this body is different from others they've found on the mountain. For one thing, it is mostly undamaged. For another, its skin is dried out, like a <u>mummy's</u>. And with it is a knife with a small stone blade.

The body turned out to be much older than the tourists could have guessed. When specialists had a chance to examine it, they discovered it had been there for about <u>five thousand years!</u>

How could a body stay preserved for all this time? Two things probably helped. First, the place where the man died was <u>somewhat sheltered, so</u> animals couldn't get at it. Then he was quickly <u>covered by falling snow.</u> Wind blowing through the snow probably "<u>freeze-dried" his body,</u> removing all moisture from it.

Objects found with the body told something about the Iceman's life. He wore a well-made fur jacket and pants. He clearly had been hunting, for he carried arrows, and animal bones were nearby. He also had a braided grass mat for sitting or sleeping on. Perhaps he was exhausted when he lay down for the last time.

The body was found in <u>1991,</u> when some of the ice on the mountain melted. Searching for the cause of the Iceman's death, scientists put the body back into cold conditions—and hoped.

Figure B: Top-Down Topic Web and Two-Column Notes

Top Down Web: Includes topic and main ideas without details

The Mysterious Iceman

| A Frozen body was found | Specialists examined it | Possetions were found |

Two Column Notes: Includes main ideas on the left and supporting details on the right

Main ideas	Supporting details
A Frozen body was found	icy mountain in the Alps of Europe.
	A Frozen body faced down in the snow
	stuck to the ice
Specialists examined it	5,000 years old
	realiced the body was in different conditions.
	faured out how the body stayed preserved for all those years.
Possetions were found	with the body was some of his belongings,
	he wore a "wellmaid" fur coat and pants, and some hunting gear.

Figure C: Questions at Different Levels of Bloom's Taxonomy

Remembering	How long had the body been there?
Understanding	Describe what the body looked like.
Applying	Act out the tourists' reaction when they first saw the frozen body.
Analyzing	Examine the objects found with the body and what they tell about the man.
Evaluating	Hypothesize why it took 5000 years before the body was found.
Creating	Imagine what happened to the man that caused him to freeze the way he did.

Figure D: Summary

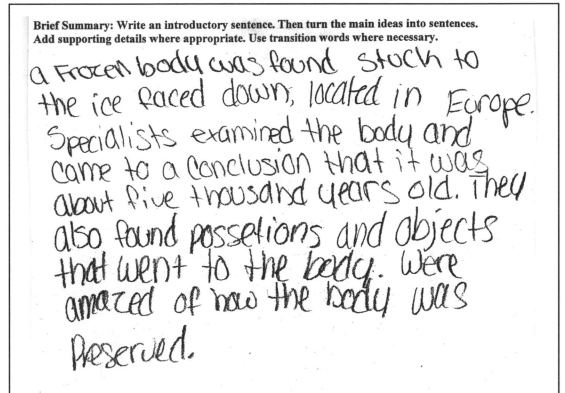

Brief Summary: Write an introductory sentence. Then turn the main ideas into sentences. Add supporting details where appropriate. Use transition words where necessary.

a Frozen body was found stuck to the ice faced down, located in Europe. Specialists examined the body and came to a conclusion that it was about five thousand years old. They also found possesions and objects that went to the body. Were amazed of how the body was Preserved.

Transition Words:
First, next, finally, before, after, during, later, also, another, in addition, similarly, however, on the contrary, most important, nevertheless, therefore, as a result, for example.....

Example 2: Social Studies – Textbook Chapter

Figure A: Top-Down Topic Web of the Full Chapter

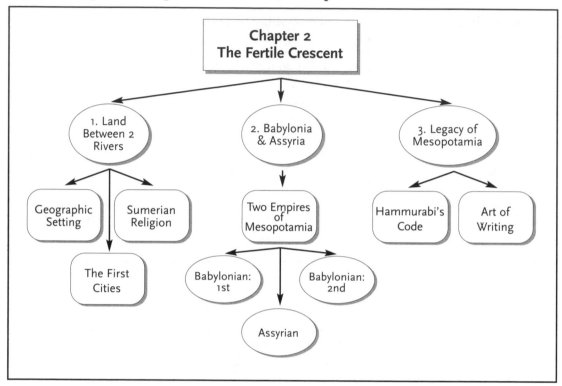

Figure B: Sub-Web from the Topic Web

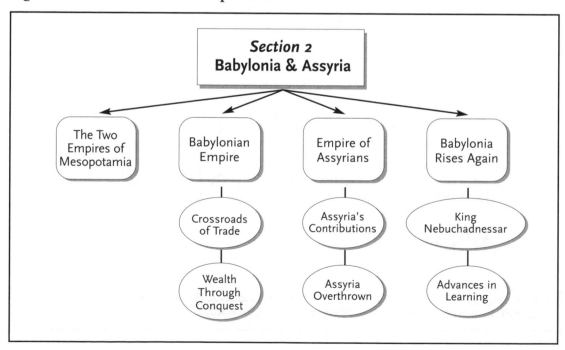

Figure C: Two-Column Notes on Section 2

Section 2: Babylonia & Assyria	

2 empires of Mesopotamia	• Mesopotamia: history of conquests
	• Empire = an area or many territories controlled by 1 government
	• Biggest empires: Babylonia & Assyria
	  * B: height of empire – 1750 B.C.
	  * A: height of empire – 600's B.C.
	• Both vicious warriors, built cities

Babylonian empire	• Created by King Hammurabi
	• From Sumer to Asia Minor (Turkey today)
	• A crossroad of trade
	  * Created system of roads – improved communication & trade
	  * Caravans (groups of travelers) stopped in B & traded in bazaars (markets)
	• Wealth through conquest
	  * Hammurabi gained great wealth through conquest
	  * B eventually conquered & destroyed

Empire of the Assyrians	• Assyrians became skilled warriors
	• Started attacking other areas in 1365 B.C., by 650 B.C. was an empire
	• Assyrian contributions
	  * Invented battering ram – weapon on wheels
	  * Slings, helmets, armor, armed chariots
	  * Large library of clay tablets
	• Assyria overthrown
	  * Many revolts against them
	  * 2 groups (Medes & Chaldeans) defeated them

Babylonia rises again	• Under Chaldeans, B became empire again in 612 B.C.
	• King Nebuchadnezzar
	  * Rebuilt city of Babylon
	  * Built giant palace w/ garden & city walls
	• Advances in learning
	  * B became center of learning & science
	  * Astronomers measured time & made calendar
	  * Farmers raised honey bees
	• B was then conquered by Persians in 539 B.C.

Figure D: Questions at Different Levels of Bloom's Taxonomy

Remembering	Name the two major empires of Mesopotamia.
Understanding	Summarize the changes in empires over time in Mesopotamia.
Applying	Make a time line showing the major events and changes in empires from 1750 B.C. to 540 B.C.
Analyzing	Compare and contrast the Babylonian and Assyrian empires. How were they the same, and how were they different?
Remembering	List at least 3 Assyrian contributions.
Understanding	Explain what King Nebuchadnezzar did to rebuild the Babylonian empire and advance learning.
Evaluating	How do you think an improved system of roads affected the Babylonian Empire?
Evaluating	Hypothesize why conquest can make an empire wealthy.
Creating	What if the Assyrian's had not become skilled warriors? How do you think history in that part of the world would have changed?

Figure E: Use of Summary Template

Summary Template

1. List the main ideas in phrase form.
- Empires by conquest
- Babylonia created by Hammurabi — crossrods of trade
- Assyrians skilled warriors — many contributions
- Babylonia empire again — center of learning and science
-

2. Write an introductory sentence that states the topic of the summary.
The two greatest empires of Mesopotamia were Babylon and Assyria.

3. Turn the main ideas into sentences using your own words. You can combine some of the main ideas into one sentence.
As a result of war and conquest these empires changed over time. The first large empire was Babylonia. It was created by King Hammurabi and was the crossroads of trade routes. Assyrians conquered Babylonia. They were skilled warriors who made many contributions. Babylonia became an empire again after Assyria was conquered. It became a center of learning and science.

4. Add transition words from the list below or from the transition poster.
first, next, finally, before, after, during, later, also, another, in addition, in conclusion, to sum up, similarly, however, on the contrary, most important, for example, as a result, therefore

5. Proofread and edit your summary.

Figure F: Summary

Section 2 Summary

The two great empires of Mesopotamia were Babylon and Assyria and both were warriors. <u>As a result</u> of war and conquest these empires changed over time. <u>The first</u> large empire was Babylonia. It was created by King Hammurabi and developed a system of roads. <u>As a result</u> it became a crossroads of trade routes. <u>The second</u> empire was the Assyrians who conquered the Babylonians. They were skilled warriors who made many contributions to civilization. <u>However</u>, they were conquered and once again Babylon became an empire. This time Babylonia became a center of learning and science.

Example 3: Science – Textbook Section

Figure A: Textbook Section

Fishes

About 540 million years ago the first fishes appeared in the Earth's oceans. These fishes were strange-looking animals, indeed! They had no jaws, and their bodies were covered by bony plates instead of scales. And although they had fins, the fins were not like those of modern-day fishes. But these early fishes were the first animals to have vertebral columns. They were the first vertebrates to have evolved.

Despite these differences, there was something special about these animals – something that would group them with the many kinds of fishes that were to follow millions of years later. Fishes are water-dwelling vertebrates that are characterized by scales, fins, and throats with gill slits. It is important to note, however, that not all fishes have all these characteristics. For example, sturgeons, paddlefishes, and sea horses have no scales at all on most of their body. And although most fishes have fins, the fins vary greatly in structure and function. Some fishes have paired fins, whereas others have single fins. Some fishes use their fins to help them remain upright. Other fishes use their fins to help them steer and stop. The side-to-side movement of large tail fins helps most fishes to move through the water. However, all fishes have gill slits.

As a group, fishes eat just about everything – from microscopic algae to worms to dead fish. The parrotfish even eats coral! Fishes have developed special structures that enable them to catch or eat the great variety of foods upon which they feed. Swordfishes are thought to slash their way through large groups of fishes and then return to devour the wounded or dead prey. Toadfishes rely on their ability to blend in with their surroundings to catch their prey. And angler fishes have wormlike lures that they dangle in front of their prey.

Like all vertebrates, fishes have a closed circulatory system. A closed circulatory system is one in which the blood is contained within the blood vessels. In fishes, the blood travels through the blood vessels in a single loop – from the heart to the gills to the rest of the body and back to the heart. The excretory system of fishes consists of tubelike kidneys that filter nitrogen-containing wastes from the blood. Like many other water-dwelling animals, most fishes get rid of the nitrogen-containing wastes in the form of ammonia. Fishes have a fairly well-developed nervous system. Almost all fishes have sense organs that collect information

---

about their environment. Most fishes that are active in daylight have eyes with color vision almost as good as yours. Those fishes that are active at night or that live in murky water have large eyes with big pupils. Do you know what this adaptation enables them to do?

Many fishes have keen senses of smell and taste. For example, sharks can detect the presence of one drop of blood in 115 liters of sea water! Although most fishes cannot hear sounds well, they can detect faint currents and vibrations in the water through a "distant-touch" system. As a fish moves, its distant-touch system responds to changes in the movement of the water, thus enabling the fish to detect prey or to avoid objects in its path.

In most species of fishes, males and females are separate individuals. The males produce sperm, and the females produce eggs. There are, however, a number of fish species that are born males but develop into females. Others begin their lives as females and then change into males. Whatever the case, few fishes function as both male and female at the same time.

Of the many fishes that lay eggs, most have external fertilization. External fertilization is the process in which a sperm joins with an egg outside the body. Certain egg-laying fishes have internal fertilization. Internal fertilization is the process in which sperm joins with an egg inside the body. Of the fishes that have internal fertilization, some – such as sharks and rays – lay fertilized eggs. In other fishes that have internal fertilization, the eggs develop inside the females body. In this case, each developing fish receives food either directly from the female or indirectly from a yolk sac attached to its body. When all the food in its yolk sac is used up, the young fish is born.

Many fishes (including some you can keep in an aquarium) have interesting mating behaviors. For example, male guppies dance in front of female guppies to get their attention. The bright red and blue body of a male three-spined stickleback serves to let female sticklebacks know where his nest is, as well as to warn other males to keep away.

The correct scientific classification of fishes is quite complicated. Thus, in this textbook fishes are placed into three main groups. These groups are the jawless fishes, the cartilaginous fishes, and the bony fishes.

(From "Exploring Life Science" © 1997 by Prentice Hall, Inc. Used by permission of Pearson Education, Inc.)

Figure B: Top-Down Topic Web

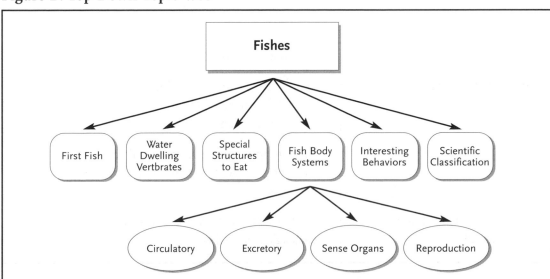

Figure C: Two-Column Notes

FISHES	
first fish appear in oceans	- 540 million years ago - strange-looking - no jaws, no scales, strange fins - were first vertebrates
fishes are water-dwelling vertebrates	- most have scales, fins, and gill slits - a few have no scales - fins vary in structure and function - all fish have gill slits
special structures to eat food	- fish eat everything - some slash way through groups of fish (swordfish) - some blend in with surroundings - some have lures to attract prey
have closed circulatory system	- blood is contained within vessels - travels in single loop
excretory system	- tubelike kidneys filter waste - excrete waste in form of ammonia
sense organs	- adapted eyes for vision - keen sense of smell and taste - detect vibrations for touch
males and females are separate	- males produce sperm, females eggs - some born as one sex, then change to other - very few function as both
external fertilization	- most fish - sperm joins with eggs outside body
internal fertilization	- sperm joins with eggs inside body - some lay fertilized eggs - some develop eggs in female and then birth
interesting behaviors	- male guppies dance to get female attention - male bright colors help females find them and keep away prey
scientific classification is complicated	- book uses 3 main groups: jawless, cartilaginous, and bony

Figure D: Questions at Different Levels of Bloom's Taxonomy

Understanding	Describe what the first fish looked like.
Applying	Draw a picture of a fish. Be sure to include scales, fins, and gill slits.
Remembering and Evaluating	Give 3 examples of special structures used to catch food. Deduce how each of these structures help fish catch food.
Applying	Illustrate how the excretory system works.
Creating	How do you think the sense organs might be different for a fish that lives in a totally dark place?
Analyzing and Evaluating	Compare and contrast external and internal fertilization. Which type of fertilization do you think is better for resulting in more young fish surviving? Justify your answer.
Understanding	Explain two examples of interesting fish behavior.
Understanding	List the 3 main classifications of fishes.

Figure E: Summary

FISHES

The first fish appeared millions of years ago. <u>*Today,*</u> *all fish are water-dwelling vertebrates and most have scales, fins, and gill slits. Fish use special structures to help them attract prey and eat.* <u>*They also*</u> *have closed circulatory systems and excretory systems.* <u>*In addition,*</u> *fish have strong sense organs to see, smell, and touch. Most fish are either male or female,* <u>*although*</u> *some can change sex or function as both. Most fish fertilize eggs outside the body.* <u>*However,*</u> *some fish fertilize eggs inside the body and then give birth to live fish. Some fish exhibit interesting behaviors.* <u>*For example,*</u> *some males dance or have bright colors. There are three main classifications of fish,* <u>*including*</u> *jawless, those with cartilage, and those with bones.*

Figure F: Use of Summary Template

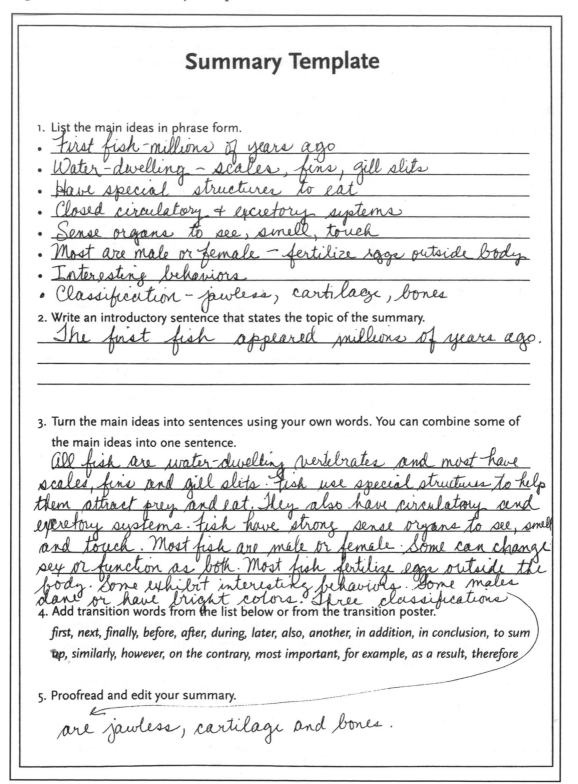

Summary Template

1. List the main ideas in phrase form.
   - First fish - millions of years ago
   - Water-dwelling - scales, fins, gill slits
   - Have special structures to eat
   - Closed circulatory & excretory systems
   - Sense organs to see, smell, touch
   - Most are male or female - fertilize eggs outside body
   - Interesting behaviors
   - Classification - jawless, cartilage, bones

2. Write an introductory sentence that states the topic of the summary.
   The first fish appeared millions of years ago.

3. Turn the main ideas into sentences using your own words. You can combine some of the main ideas into one sentence.
   All fish are water-dwelling vertebrates and most have scales, fins and gill slits. Fish use special structures to help them attract prey and eat. They also have circulatory and excretory systems. Fish have strong sense organs to see, smell and touch. Most fish are male or female. Some can change sex or function as both. Most fish fertilize eggs outside the body. Some exhibit interesting behaviors. Some males dance or have bright colors. Three classifications

4. Add transition words from the list below or from the transition poster.
   first, next, finally, before, after, during, later, also, another, in addition, in conclusion, to sum up, similarly, however, on the contrary, most important, for example, as a result, therefore

5. Proofread and edit your summary.
   are jawless, cartilage and bones.

Example 4: Math – Chapter Section About Triangles

Figure A: Top-Down Topic Web

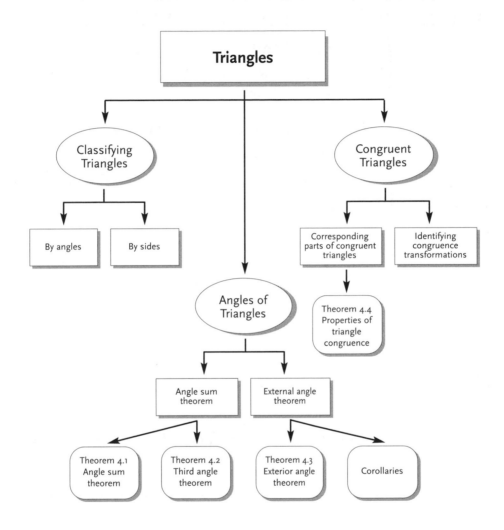

Figure B: Two Column Notes

Classifying Triangles

by angles	• all triangles have at least 2 acute angles
	• the third angle is used to classify
	• acute triangle = all angles are acute (all measure < 90)
	• obtuse triangle = one angle is obtuse (1 measures > 90)
	• right triangle = one angle is right (1 measures 90)
by sides	• equal number hash marks to show congruent
	• scalene triangle = no 2 sides same
	• isosceles triangle = 2 sides same
	• equilateral triangle = all sides same

Figure C: Summary

There are two ways to classify triangles. The <u>first</u> is by angles. All the angles measure less than 90 in an acute triangle. In an obtuse triangle one angle measures greater than 90. <u>Finally</u>, in a right triangle, one angle equals 90. The <u>second</u> way to classify is by sides. No two sides of a scalene triangle are the same. In an isosceles triangle, two sides are the same. In an equilateral triangle, all sides are the same.

Figure D: Questions at Different Levels of Bloom's Taxonomy

Remembering	Identify the two ways to classify triangles.
Understanding	Describe an acute triangle and an equilateral triangle.
Applying	Draw an example of a right triangle.
Analyzing	Categorize the following kinds of triangles by side or angle: acute, equilateral, isosceles, obtuse, right angle, scalene.
Evaluating	Which type of triangle would be best for the roof of a house in a snowy climate? In a desert? Justify your answer.
Creating	Design furniture for a house that incorporates each of the six types of triangles.

Chapter 6

Implementing the Routine Across a School

The Key Comprehension Routine can be used: in an individual classroom; by a team of teachers; across classrooms in a single content area (e.g., science, social studies, or math); and/or by specialists (e.g., reading and special education teachers). Ideally, however, *The Key Comprehension Routine* should be part of a school-wide model for addressing content literacy in intermediate, middle, and high school grades.

As previously noted, exposure to effective strategy instruction in just one classroom will support reading comprehension. When students are exposed to consistent strategy instruction in multiple classrooms, however, they are likely to learn comprehension strategies more quickly and thoroughly. Exposure to strategy instruction over several grades in different content areas results in more independent use of strategies. To ensure the sort of consistency in strategies that produces strong improvement in comprehension, we recommend school-wide adoption of *The Key Comprehension Routine*.

As most administrators know, school-wide change and the adoption of a new instructional program can be overwhelming for teachers. In some cases, it may be best to pilot *The Key Comprehension Routine* with one team of teachers or across one grade level. The model can be expanded gradually to other teams of teachers and grades. Once one team of teachers experiences positive results from incorporating the routine, other teachers are more willing to adopt it. As with all new programs, it may take several years of commitment by faculty and administrators combined with follow-up professional development for *The Key Comprehension Routine* to become an established, lasting part of a school-wide literacy curriculum.

Support Components

There are several components that facilitate school-wide implementation of *The Key Comprehension Routine*:

* **Strong leadership.** A commitment from school administrators to provide ongoing support for implementation of *The Key Comprehension Routine* is essential. Administrators must become knowledgeable about the program, and it is also helpful to attend initial training with the faculty. This level of participation conveys to teachers that the eventual goal is the program's integration as a building initiative.

* **Involvement of all faculty.** Many teachers already incorporate some type of comprehension strategy instruction. The advantage of The Key Comprehension Routine is that it offers a flexible model for strategy instruction that is consistent as students move from class to class and grade to grade. Teachers must be willing to adapt their instruction practices to include the activities of The Key

Comprehension Routine to remain consistent with other teachers. This requires a willingness to share ideas and sample assignments with peers. It is important to include all faculty members (i.e., content classroom teachers, specialists, paraprofessionals) in the professional development.

✳ **Quality initial and long-term professional development.** Initial training that provides opportunities for teachers to practice generating classroom lessons and activities using their own content reading material is essential, and this professional development should be provided by Keys to Literacy trainers. Initial training should be followed by long-term building based, professional development that includes guided practice time, small-group peer sharing, and classroom observation and feedback.

✳ **Key Comprehension Routine building coaches.** Several individuals should be identified and trained as building-based coaches. A Key Comprehension building coach can be a literacy specialist, administrator, curriculum coordinator, department chair, content classroom teacher, or any other faculty member who supports the program. The job of the building coach is to support teachers as they integrate *The Key Comprehension Routine*. Building coaches can facilitate guided practice sessions, small-group sharing meetings, or classroom observations.

✳ **Common meeting time.** Communication, especially among teachers who work with the same students, is key to successful school-wide implementation of *The Key Comprehension Routine*. Teachers should meet by team, grade level, or subject department at least once per month to share how they are using the strategy activities in their classroom. Building-based coaches can facilitate these meetings. Keys to Literacy offers *Implementation Folders* that teachers use to save sample lesson plans and student work to share during common meeting time. If it is possible, content teachers from the same department should be given common planning time to develop strategy activities for shared content topics.

✳ **Formalize the routine.** If the goal of professional development for *The Key Comprehension Routine* is its adoption as a school-wide program, it must be formally identified as a building initiative. Parents and the community should be made aware of the activities in the routine, and a process to train new teachers should be created. It is also helpful to communicate with teachers of earlier grades in order to familiarize them with the strategy instruction their students will later receive. Likewise, it is helpful to communicate with teachers in later grades so they will be better able to support student use of the skills in their classrooms.

✳ **The importance of organizational skills.** Many students do not have the organizational skills required to set up and maintain a system for organizing their class papers, homework, books, and materials. To support strategy instruction, students benefit from using a notebook routine to organize the topic webs, two-column notes, summaries, and question generation activities they will generate.

The Key Notebook Routine (Sedita, 1989, 1999) is one example of a formal routine for sorting, storing, and cleaning out notebooks on a regular basis. It also includes a daily and long-term calendar system for planning homework and long-term assignments. More information about The Key Notebook Routine is available at the Keys to Literacy website (www.keystoliteracy.com).

NOTES:

Review Activities

Part 1

<u>Directions</u>: *Review the major components of The Key Comprehension Routine. Take notes under each question.*

Main Idea Skills
What is it?
What did I learn about how to teach it?
How can I use it this month?
Top-Down Topic Webs
What is it?
What did I learn about how to teach it?
How can I use it this month?

Two-Column Notes

What is it?

What did I learn about how to teach it?

How can I use it this month?

Summary

What is it?

What did I learn about how to teach it?

How can I use it this month?

Question Generation
What is it?
What did I learn about how to teach it?
How can I use it this month?

Part 2

<u>*Directions*</u>*: Answer the questions.*

How will *The Key Comprehension Routine* change my teaching?

_____

_____

_____

_____

_____

_____

_____

_____

_____

How will *The Key Comprehension Routine* change my students?

_____

_____

_____

_____

_____

_____

_____

_____

_____

_____

Reproducible Templates

The Key Comprehension Routine

Components	Specifics
Main Idea Skills and Text Structure	• Identifying and stating main ideas • Categorizing • Paragraph level main ideas • Text structure
Activity 1: Top-Down Topic Webs	• Based on reading • Based on instructional topic • Before writing
Activity 2: Two-Column Notes	• Detailed notes • Big-picture notes
Activity 3: Summary	• Limited summary • Big-picture summary
Activity 4: Question Generation	• Using main ideas from text headings, topic webs, notes • Levels of questions using Bloom's Taxonomy

Finding the Main Idea

1. Identify the details.
2. Compare the details to determine what they have in common.
3. Use your own words to paraphrase what they have in common.

Techniques

Goldilocks

- Is my main idea too specific?
- Is my main idea too general?
- How can I change it so it is just right?

Labeling the Bucket

- What label for the bucket describes what is inside?

Self-Cuing

- The topic is _____
- What is the paragraph saying about the topic?_____

Two-Column Notes

Date: _____

Topic: _____

Main Ideas	Details

Note Editing Steps

✳   Check to be sure that all the main ideas are listed and clearly stated in the left column.

✳   Check to be sure that all key details are in the right column. If there is irrelevant information, cross it out.

✳   Ask the teacher or another student to provide any missing information.

✳   If necessary, reduce wording into more concise phrases.

✳   Expand abbreviations and wording if the notes are unclear.

✳   Add visual markers (for example: horizontal lines, arrows, or numbers) to further organize notes.

✳   Make sure all note pages are dated and in order.

How To Write A Summary

1. Read the material and identify the main ideas. Distinguish the main ideas from the details.

2. Write the main ideas in phrase form.

3. Begin the summary with an introductory statement.

4. Turn the main ideas into sentences, occasionally including details when it is necessary to convey the main idea.

5. Combine the sentences into one or more paragraphs.

6. Use transition words to connect the sentences and the paragraphs.

7. Proofread the summary for punctuation, spelling, sentence structure, and content.

Summary Template

1. List the main ideas in phrase form.

   - _____
   - _____
   - _____
   - _____
   - _____
   - _____
   - _____

2. Write an introductory sentence that states the topic of the summary.

   _____
   _____
   _____

3. Turn the main ideas into sentences using your own words. You can combine some of the main ideas into one sentence.

   _____
   _____
   _____
   _____
   _____
   _____
   _____
   _____
   _____
   _____
   _____
   _____
   _____
   _____
   _____
   _____

4. Add transition words from the list below or from the transition poster.
   first, next, finally, before, after, during, later, also, another, in addition, in conclusion, to sum up, similarly, however, on the contrary, most important, for example, as a result, therefore

5. Proofread and edit your summary.

Transition Words and Phrases

To indicate a time relationship	after, afterward, after that, at first, at this time, before, beginning with, beyond, during, earlier, ending with, eventually, finally, following, from then on, in the meantime, last, later, meanwhile, next, now, since, soon, then, until, while
To indicate spatial placement	below, beside, between, beyond, farther on, here, next to, parallel with
To list or present a series of ideas	after, after that, finally, first, lastly, next, second, third
To add information or continue a line of thought	also, another, besides, further, furthermore, in addition, likewise, moreover, similarly
To summarize or show conclusion	accordingly, finally, in conclusion, in other words, in short, to conclude, to sum up, to summarize
To show comparison	by comparison, compared to, in like manner, likewise, similarly
To show contrast	although, but, however, in contrast, nevertheless, on the contrary, on the other hand, unlike
To repeat information or stress a point	above all, in fact, in other words, most important, once again, to repeat
To provide an example or illustrate a point	for example, for instance, such as, to illustrate, that is
To show cause and effect	as a result, because, because of, caused by, consequently, for that reason, that is why, therefore, thus
To state the obvious	certainly, granted that, in fact, most certainly, naturally, obviously, of course, surely, undoubtedly, without a doubt

Bloom's Taxonomy

Creating: *what if? create*

Evaluating: *fair/unfair; right/wrong; ranking*

Analyzing: *compare/contrast*

Applying: *life and use*

Understanding: *in your own words*

Remembering: *facts*

Question Terms

Remembering	Understanding	Applying	Analyzing	Evaluating	Creating
Cite	Describe	Adapt	Analyze	Appraise	Assemble
Define	Discuss	Apply	Arrange	Assess	Compile
Find	Explain	Compute	Categorize	Choose	Compose
Give an example	Interpret	Demonstrate	Compare	Conclude	Concoct
Identify	Paraphrase	Dramatize	Contrast	Criticize	Construct
Label	Report	Draw	Deconstruct	Critique	Create
List	Restate in own words	Illustrate	Detect	Debate	Design
Locate	Retell	Implement	Dissect	Deduce	Develop
Match	Review	Interview	Distinguish	Defend	Devise
Name	Summarize	Make	Examine	Hypothesize	Formulate
Quote	Translate	Operate	Group	Judge	Generate
Recall		Practice	Inspect	Justify	Imagine
Recite		Role play	Integrate	Prioritize	Invent
Recognize		Sequence	Organize	Rank	Make
Retrieve		Solve	Probe	Rate	Originate
Show		Use	Research	Reject	Prepare
			Separate	Validate	Produce
			Sift		Set up
					What if?

Adapted from Bloom, 1956, and Anderson and Krathwhohl, 2001

Question Prompts

Level	Prompts
Remembering	Where is... What did... Who was... When did... How many... Locate it in the story... Point to the...
Understanding	Tell me in your own words... What does it mean... Give me an example of... Describe what... Make a map of... What is the main idea of...
Applying	What would happen to you if... Would you have done the same as... If you were there, would you... How would you solve the problem... In the library, find information about...
Analyzing	What things would you have used... What other ways could... What things are similar/different? What things couldn't have happened in real life? What kind of person is... What caused _____ to act the way she/he did?
Evaluating	Would you recommend this book? Why? Why not? Select the best...Why is it the best? What do you think will happen to... Why do you think that? Rank the events in order of importance. Which character would you most like to meet? Why? Was _____ good or bad? Why Did you like the story? Why?
Creating	What would it be like if... What would it be like to live... Design a... Pretend you are a... What would have happened if... Why/why not? Use your imagination to draw a picture of... Add a new item on your own... Tell/write a different ending...

Adapted from: Fisher, D.B., and Frey, N. (2007). "Checking for Understanding." Alexandria, VA: ASCD.

References

References

Alfassi, M. (2004). Reading to learn: Effects of combined strategy instruction on high school students. *Journal of Educational Research, 97(4),* 171-184.

Alvermann, D.E. and Moore, D. (1991). Secondary school reading. In R. Barr, M.L. Kamil, P. Mosenthal, and P.D. Pearson (eds.) *Handbook of Reading Research 2:* 951-983. White Plains, NY: Longman.

Anderson, L.W., Karthwhohl, D.R. (Eds.) (2001). *A Taxonomy for Learning, Teaching and Assessing: A Revision of Bloom's Taxonomy of Educational Objectives.* New York: Addison-Wesley Longman.

Anderson, V., and Hidi, S. (1988-1989). Teaching students to summarize. *Educational Leadership 46:* 26-28.

Beck, I, and McKeown, M. (1981). Developing questions that promote comprehension: The story map. *Language Arts (November/December),* 913-918.

Beck, I.L., McKeown, M.G., Hamilton, R.L., and Kucan, L. (1997). *Questioning the author: An approach for enhancing student engagement with text.* Newark, DE: International Reading Association.

Biancarosa, G., and Snow, C.E. (2004). *Reading next: A vision for action and research in middle and high school literacy: A report from Carnegie Corporation of New York.* Washington, DC: Alliance for Excellent Education.

Bloom B. S. (1956). *Taxonomy of educational objectives, Handbook I: The cognitive domain.* New York: David McKay Co Inc.

Brody, S. (2001). Comprehension: Gathering information and constructing understanding, and Previews: Learning pertinent background and text concepts. In S. Brody (ed.), *Teaching reading: Language, letters, and thought,* 213-253. Milford, NH: LARC Publishing.

Carlisle, J. and Rice, M. (2002). *Improving reading comprehension: Research-based principles and practices.* Baltimore: York Press.

Chall, J. (1996). *Stages of reading development* (2nd ed.). Orlando, FL: Harcourt Brace.

Curtis, M.E., and Longo, A.M. (1999). *When adolescents can't read.* Manchester, NH: Brookline Books.

Curtis, M.E. (2002). *Adolescent reading: A synthesis of research.* Presentation at the conference "Adolescent Literacy – Research Informing Practice: A Series of Workshops." May 20, 2002, Baltimore. Sponsored by The Partnership for Reading.

Dickson. S.V., Simmons, D. C., and Kame'enui, E.J. (1995). *Text organization: Curricular and instructional implications for diverse learners.* Eugene, OR: National Center to Improve the Tools of Educators.

Dole, J.A., Brown, K.J., & Trathen, W. (1996). The effects of strategy instruction on the comprehension performance of at-risk students. *Reading Research Quarterly, 31,* 62-88.

Duke, N. K., Pressley, M., and Hilden, K. (2004). Difficulties with reading comprehension. In C.A. Stone, E.R. Silliman, B.J. Ehren, and K. Apel (eds.). *Handbook of language and literacy: Development and disorders,* 501-520. New York: Guilford Press.

Fisher, D.B. and Frey, N. (2007). *Checking for understanding.* Alexandria, VA: ASCD.

Forbes, E. (1943). *Johnny Tremain.* Boston: Houghton Mifflin.

Gambrell, L.B., and Bales, R.J. (1986). Mental imagery and the comprehension-monitoring performance of fourth and fifth-grade poor readers. *Reading Research Quarterly, 21,* 454-464.

Gaskins, I.W. (1998). There's more to teaching at-risk and delayed readers than good reading instruction. *The Reading Teacher, 51(7),* 534-547.

Golding, William (1954). *Lord of the flies.* United Kingdom: Faber and Faber.

Graham, S., & Hebert. M.A. (2010). *Writing to read: Evidence for how writing can improve reading. A Carnegie Corporation Time to Act Report.* Washington, DC: Alliance for Excellent Education.

Graham, S., & Perin, D. (2007). *Writing next: Effective strategies to improve the writing of adolescents in middle and high schools – A report to Carnegie Corporation of New York.* Washington, DC: Alliance for Excellent Education.

Guthrie, J.T., & Humenick, N.M. (2004). Motivating students to read: Evidence for classroom practices that increase reading motivation and achievement. In P. McCardle & V. Chhabra (Eds.). *The voice of evidence in reading research* (pp. 213-234). Baltimore: Brookes.

Heller, H. and Greenleaf, C. (2007). *Literacy instruction in the content areas: Getting to the core of middle and high school improvement.* Washington, D.C. Alliance for Excellent Education.

Kamil, M.L., Borman, G.D., Dole, J., Kral, C.C., Salinger, T., & Torgesen, J. (2008). *Improving adolescent literacy: Effective classroom and intervention practices: A Practice Guide* (NCEE #2008-4027). Washington, D.C.: National Center for Education and Evaluation and Regional Assistance, Institute of Education Sciences, U.S. Department of Education. Retrieved from http://ies.ed.gov.ncee.wwc.

Klingner, J.K., Vaughn, S. and Schumm, J.S. (1998). Collaborative strategic reading during social studies in heterogeneous fourth-grade classrooms. *Elementary School Journal. 99 (1)*, 3-22.

Klingner, J.K., Vaughn, S., Dimino, J., Schumm, J.S., and Bryant, D. (2001). *Collaborative strategic reading: Strategies for improving comprehension.* Longmont, CO: Sopris West Educational Services.

Klingner, J.K., and Vaughn, S. (2004). Strategies for struggling second-language readers. In T.L. Jetton and J.A. Dole, eds., *Adolescent literacy: Research and practice.* New York: Guildford Press.

Lehr, F., Osborn, J., Hiebert, E.H. (2005). *A focus on comprehension.* Honolulu, HI: Pacific Resources for Education and Learning.

Lysynchuk, L.M., Pressley, M., & Vye, N.J. (1990). Reciprocal teaching improves standardized reading-comprehension performance in poor comprehenders. *The Elementary School Journal, 90,* 469-484.

Maria, K. (1990). *Reading comprehension instruction: Issues and strategies.* Parkton, MD: York Press.

Meltzer, J., Smith, N.C., and Clark, H. (2003). *Adolescent literacy resources: Linking research and practice.* Providence, R.I.: Northeast and Islands Regional Educational Laboratory at Brown University.

Moats, L. C. (2001). When older kids can't read. *Educational Leadership, March 2001.*

Moje, E.B. (2006). Motivating texts, motivating contexts, motivating adolescents: An examination of the role of motivation in adolescent literacy practices and development. *Perspectives, 32,* 10-14.

National Reading Panel. (2000). *Teaching children to read: An evidence-based assessment of the scientific research literature on reading and its implications for reading instruction.* Washington, DC: National Institute of Child Health and Human Development.

Noles, J.D. and Dole, J.A. (2004). Helping adolescent readers through explicit strategy instruction. In T.L. Jetton and J.A. Dole (eds.). *Adolescent literacy research and practice.* New York: Guilford Press.

Ogle, D. (1986). The K-W-L: A teaching model that develops active reading of expository text. *The Reading Teacher, 45 (4),* 298-306.

Ogle, D.M. (1989). The know, want to know, learning strategy. In K.D. Muth (ed.), *Children's comprehension of text,* 205-223. Newark, DE: International Reading Association.

Palinscar, A.S., and Brown, A.L. (1985). Reciprocal teaching: Activities to promote 'reading with your mind'. In T.L. Harris and E.J. Cooper (eds.), *Reading, thinking, and concept development*, 147-158. New York: College Board Publications.

Palinscar, A.S. and Brown, A.L. (1984). Reciprocal teaching of comprehension-fostering and comprehension-monitoring activities. *Cognition and Instruction, 1*, 117-175.

Pauk, W. (1997). *How to study in college (7th ed)*. Boston: Houghton Mifflin.

Paulson, G. (1987). *Hatchet*. NY: Scholastic.

Pearson, P.E., and Gallagher, M.C. (1983). The instruction of reading comprehension. *Contemporary Educational Psychology, 8*, 317-344.

Peterson, C.L., Caverly, D. C., Nicholson, S.A., O'Neill, S., and Cusenbary, S. (2000). *Building reading proficiency at the secondary level*. Austin, TX: Southwest Educational Development Laboratory.

Pressley, M. (2000). What should comprehension instruction be the instruction of? In M. Kamil, Mosenthal, P., Pearson, P.D. and Barr, R. (eds.), *Handbook of reading research, 3*: 545-561. Hillsdale, NJ: Erlbaum.

Raphael, T.E. (1982). Question-answering strategies for children. *The Reading Teacher, 36*, 186-190.

Raphael, T.E. (1986). Teaching question-answer relationships, revisited. *The Reading Teacher, 39*, 516-522.

Rosenshine, B., Meister, C., and Chapman, S. (1996). Teaching students to generate questions: A review of the intervention studies. *Reviews of Educational Research, 66 (2)*, 181-221.

Samuels, S.J. (2002). Reading fluency: Its development and assessment. In Pacific Resources for Education and Learning (Ed.), *Readings on fluency for "A focus on fluency forum."* Honolulu, HI: PREL.

Sedita, J. (1989). *Landmark study skills guide*. Prides Crossing, MA: Landmark School Press.

Sedita, J. (1999). Organizational strategies: The master notebook system. *Their World, 1998/1999 annual edition*. New York: National Center for Learning Disabilities.

Sedita, J. (2001). *Study Skills* (2nd ed.). Prides Crossing, MA: Landmark School Press.

Sedita, J. (2003, 2009). *The Key Vocabulary Routine.* Rowley, MA: Keys to Literacy.

Shankweiler, D., Lundquist, E., Katz, L., Stuebing, K.K., Fletcher, J.M., Brady, S., Fowler, A., Dreyer, L.G., Marchione, K.E., Shaywitz, S.E., and Shaywitz, B.A. (1999). Comprehension and decoding: Patterns of association in children with reading difficulties. *Scientific Studies of Reading, 31.*

Snow, C. (2002). (Chair). *RAND reading study group: Reading for understanding: Toward an R&D program in reading comprehension.* Santa Monica, CA: RAND.

Snow, C., Griffin, P., & Burns, M.S. (Eds.)(2005). *Knowledge to support the teaching of reading: Preparing teachers for a changing world.* San Francisco: Jossey-Bass.

Snow-Renner, R., & Lauer, P.A. (2005). *Professional development analysis.* Denver, CO: Mid-continent Research for Education Learning.

Stahl, S.A. (1999). *Vocabulary development.* Newton Upper Falls, MA: Brookline Books.

Sweet, A.P., and Snow, C.E. (2003) (eds.). *Rethinking reading comprehension.* New York: Guilford Press.

Tomlinson, C.A. (2003) Differentiating instruction for academic diversity. In J.M. Cooper (Ed.), *Classroom teaching skills, 7th ed., 149-180.* Boston: Houghton Mifflin.

Torgesen, J.K., Houston, D.D., Rissman, L.M., Decker, S.M., Roberts, G., Vaughn, S., Wexler, J., Francis, D.J., Rivera, M.O., Lesaux, N. (2007). *Academic literacy instruction for adolescents: A guidance document from the Center on Instruction.* Portsmouth, NH: RMC Research Corporation, Center on Instruction.

Trabasso, T., & Bouchard, E. (2002). Teaching readers how to comprehend text strategically. In C.C. Block & M. Pressley (Eds.) *Comprehension instruction: Research-based best practices.* New York: The Guilford Press.

Williams, J.P. (2002). Using the theme scheme to improve story comprehension. In C.C. Block and M. Pressley (eds.) *Comprehension instruction: Research-based best practices.* New York: Guildford Press.

Content Classroom Examples

Social Studies and History Examples

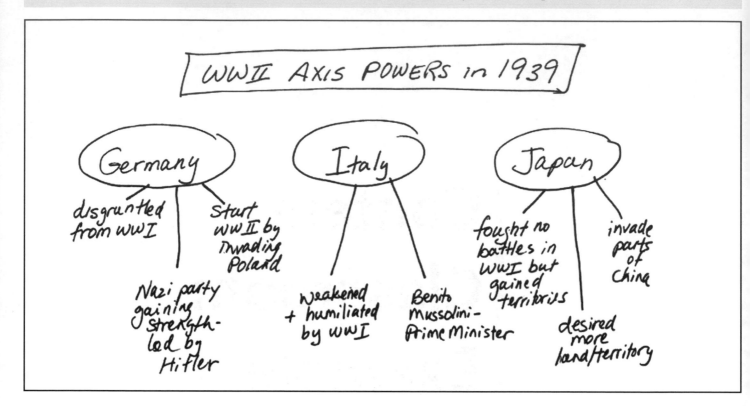

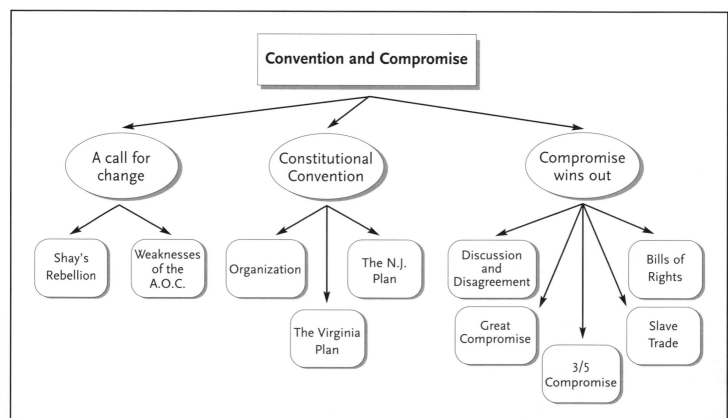

The Transportation Revolution

Heading	Notes
Before the Revolution	- 1790 - nearly 4 million people live in the United States - most people lived close to the Atlantic Ocean - 1820 - population is 10 million people so people begin to settle west of the Appalachians - A trip from New York City to Buffalo, New York took 3 weeks
Roads and Turnpikes	- In the early 1800's the Nation need good, well maintain roads - Turnpikes were privately owned roads - Travelers needed to pay to use the turnpikes - Between 1806 and 1818 a National Road is built that runs from Maryland to Vandalia, Illinois
River Travel	- 2 dis advantages to River Travel [Robert Fulton design a steam boat that can travel upstream] [One advantage of river travel is that it is more comfortable.] [Steam boat Allow transportation easier and cheap and quicker to transport] - Its difficult and slow to go upstream - most rivers in the East flow from N-S not E-W - Jame Rumsey and John Fitch design steam powered boats first
Canals	- Steam boats depended on the existing river system -Erie Canal is begun in 1873 - De Witt Clinton suggest to join Great Lakes with New York City area with canals -Erie Canal is finished in 1825 - A series of locks is designed to raise and lower boat traffic along Erie canal -Canals provide E-W travel - By 1850, the U.S. has 3600 miles of canals opening up the West to trade and settlement
Results of the Revolution	- Two waves of westward settlement (1791-1803) (1816-1821) - The 9 new states were: Vermont, Kentucky, Tennessee, Ohio, Indiana, Illinois, Mississippi, Alabama, Missouri
	- Advances in transportation over roads and waterways made western settlement possible

CHAPTER 6, SECTION 1 - EARLY BATTLES OF THE REVOLUTION
--NOTES AND REVIEW--

DIRECTIONS: This section describes three early battles;
Fort Ticonderoga, Bunker Hill and Quebec. Each of these
battles is a main idea below. Fill in details about each
battle. Then, write a summary paragraph about all three
battles.

FORT TICONDEROGA
(page 160)

- located at the southern tip of Lake Champlain
- Ethan Allen lead a band of Vermonters made a surprised attack on Fort Ticonderoga

BUNKER HILL
(page 162)

- there were 1,200 minute men
- there were 2,400 redcoast
- the Bristh won
- it was the first major battle of the Revolution.

QUEBEC
(page 164)

- Richard Montgomery & Benedict Arnold led the two first goups into Quebec.
- Dec 31 1775 they attacked Quebec and Montgomery got killed and Arnold got hurt.
- So they bristh took over Quebec.

SUMMARY (Finish this paragraph, please)

Three important early battles of the revolution were
the battles at Fort Ticonderoga, Bunker Hill, and Quebec.
In Each battle, the Americans went and tried
to take over the places. They succed in Fort Ticonderoga
and Bunker Hill. When they went to Quebec, it was very
hard to fight because of the snow storm.

Remembering	Define citizenship.
Understanding	Describe what it means to be a "good citizen."
Applying	Identify two "good citizens" in your school, community. What characteristics make them "good citizens?"
Analyzing	How does the Massachusetts Constitution compare to the U.S. Constitution?
Evaluating	Rank and justify your ranking of the rights of citizens in the following: Democracy Dictatorship Absolute monarchy Theocracy
Creating	Create a list of reasons why citizens should vote in a local or national election.

R: Locate the name and the picture that was Jean Francois's favorite animal.

U: Explain why Jean Francois studied books about Egypt.

AP: Write an interview with Jean Francois asking him 3 questions about his discovery.

AN: Contrast the Rosetta Stone and our alphabet.

E: Justify why the hieroglyph for sandals would be a good symbol for Jean Francois.

C: Create a hieroglyph that would represent you.

Northeast Coastline	· all but two NE states share borders with atlantic ocean
	· Maine to chesapeak bay
	· most reconized coastline.
Maine	· lakes
	· ME known for beatiful shore
	· rocky coast
	· skiing
	· Acadia national park
	· photogaphers and painters.
Cape Cod	· well known for fishing
	· peninsula
	· great vaitiont spots
	· very cold
	· wood's hole
	· cape cod canal
New Jersey	· Thousands of vacationers
	· valleyball, swim, relax in sun
	· atlandic city

Lindsay   1/30/09
Soacil Studies
GRADE 4

The Northeast Coastline has ~~many cool things to see~~ All but two Northeast states (Pensilvaina & Vermont) share their borders with the Northeast Coastline. The coastline starts in Maine and ends at Chesapeke Bay. It is the the most reconized coastline. In Maine it is known for it's beautiful shores. Many painters and photographers like to work there. In Cape Cod it is well known for fishing, and a good vacation spot. Im New Jersey the Coastline is another good place for a vacation and thousands of vacationers go there. This is what I know about the Northeast Coastline

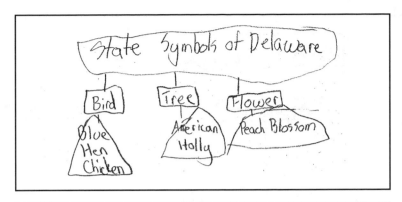

State Symbols of Delaware

- Bird — Blue Hen Chicken
- Tree — American Holly
- Flower — Peach Blossom

Delaware

- adopted April 14, 1939

bird
Blue Hen
Chicken
- fought a lot

- found in jungles of India

- plumage is gold, red, brown, dark maroon, orange, a bit of metallic green and gray, white, olive. Two white patches shaped like an ear either side of head. Distinguished by other chickens with white patches and grayish fee

tree
American Holly
- in Delaware can reach a maximum of 60 feet high and trunk has a diameter of 20 inche
- adopted May 1, 1939
- often called Christmas Holly or Evergreen Holl

- thorny leaved foliage and red berries

flower a
Peach Blossom
- adopted May 9, 1895
- alternate, simple, lanceolate, serrated,
leaf: 6 inches long, often curved along midrib,
shiny dark green above, paler below
- flower: Light Pink, carmine, to purplish,
1 inch in diameter, single seed inside superior

Delaware

State Bird
Blue Hen Chicken

The state bird of Delaware is the Blue Hen Chicken. It became the state bird on April 14, 1939. The Blue Hen Chicken is a colorful chicken, its plumage is gold, red, brown, dark maroon, orange, with a bit of metallic green and gray, white, and olive. Two white patches shaped like an ear are on either side of its head. It is found in jungles of India. The Blue Hen Chicken is native to its state. Those are some of the facts about the Blue Hen Chicken.

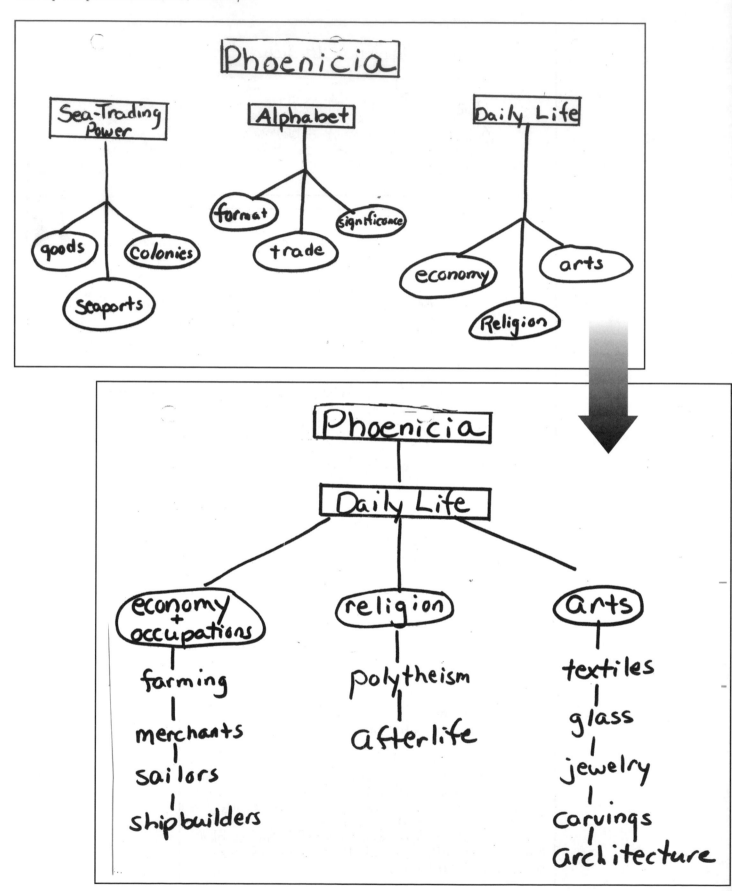

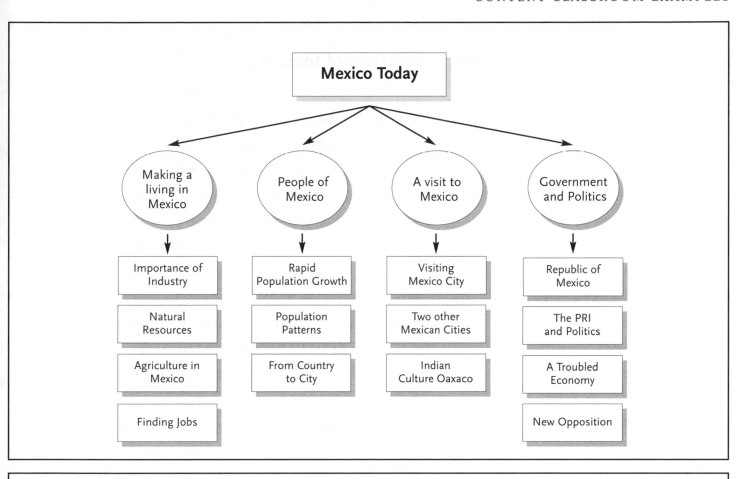

Making a Living in Mexico

• What kind of industry is in Mexico?	
• What natural resources can be found in Mexico?	
• What role does agriculture play in Mexico?	
• Is it easy or hard to find jobs in Mexico? Why?	

The Importance of Industry

1. Mexico is one of most industrialized countries in Latin America	•. Factories make many things: iron, steel, glass, chemicals, paper, cement, textiles, electrical equip, processed foods • Auto manufacturing is major industry • Manufacturing means making of goods on large scale, especially by machines
2. Manufacturing covers big area	• Stretches from Veracruz on east coast • To Guadalajara near western side • Mexico City, Puebla, Cuernavaca, Toluca, & Leon are in manufacturing area
3. Tourism is big business	• 10% of GNP came from tourism • GNP is total value of nations' goods & services produced in 1 year • To attract tourists: weather & scenery, hotel/restaurant ads, tourist agencies, efficient transportation

Importance of Industry

Mexico is one of the most industrialized countries of Latin America. Mexico manufactures many things in it factories including automobiles. The factories can be found all over the country. Another major business in Mexico is tourism. Tourism is strong *because* of the good weather and scenery. In addition, Mexico promotes tourism.

Science Examples

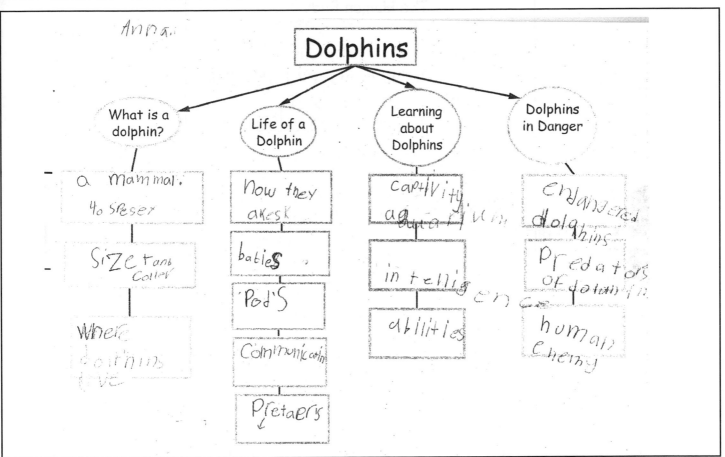

Annai

Dolphins

- **What is a dolphin?**
  - a mammal. 40 spesex
  - Size and coller
  - Where dolthins live

- **Life of a Dolphin**
  - now they akesk
  - baties
  - Pod'S
  - Communicatin
  - Pretaeris

- **Learning about Dolphins**
  - Captivity aquarium
  - intelligence
  - abilities

- **Dolphins in Danger**
  - endangered dolphins
  - Predators of dolphin
  - human enemy

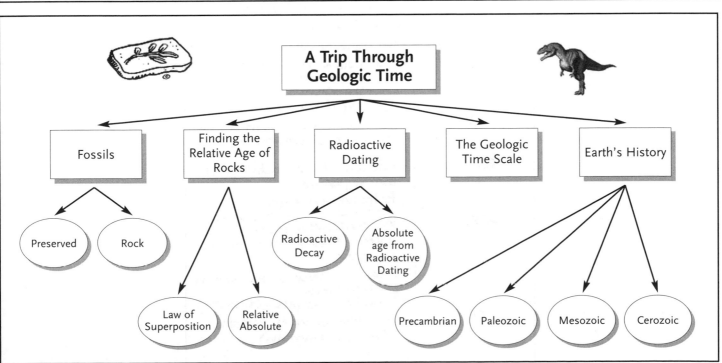

A Trip Through Geologic Time

- **Fossils**
  - Preserved
  - Rock
- **Finding the Relative Age of Rocks**
  - Law of Superposition
  - Relative Absolute
- **Radioactive Dating**
  - Radioactive Decay
  - Absolute age from Radioactive Dating
- **The Geologic Time Scale**
- **Earth's History**
  - Precambrian
  - Paleozoic
  - Mesozoic
  - Cerozoic

Name DOM

The Human Body

Main Idea	Details
A Healthy Diet	Nutrients: parts of food your body uses Water: most important Proteins: builds muscles Carbohydrates: provide main source of energy Fats: stored energy Vitamins: A,b,c,d, k,e keeps you healthy Minerals: need to keep you healthy

---

★ TYPES of FOSSILS ★

PETRIFIED	def. minerals replace all or part of the organism ex. petrified wood
MOLDS/CASTS	- the most common fossils mold: hollow area in sediment in the shape of an organism cast: copy of the shape
CARBON FILMS	- thin coating of carbon or rock in shape of organism
TRACE	- evidence of the activities of an organism - footprint in rock
AMBER	- hardened resin/sap - insects trapped - preserves whole organism
TAR	- organism stuck in tar, which preserves bones ex. La Brea tar pits (California)
ICE	- freezing preserves remains (wooly mammoth)

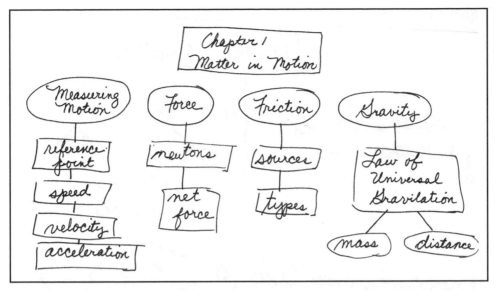

Measuring Motion

reference point	• an object that appears to stay in place compared to a moving object • we cannot observe motion without a reference point
speed	• the rate (how fast) which an object moves • need to know total distance and total time • avg. speed = $\dfrac{\text{total distance}}{\text{total time}}$

velocity	• an object's speed in a particular direction
	• a change in speed is a change in direction = a change in velocity
	• combining velocities
	  • two velocities in same direction — add
	  • two velocities in opposite directions — subtract AND take the direction of larger velocity

acceleration	• a change in velocity
	  • a change in speed OR
	  • a change in direction
	• acceleration = $\dfrac{\text{final velocity} - \text{starting velocity}}{\text{time it takes to change}}$

Water Cycle

1) Sun causes water to evaporate

2) In atmosphere, water (H₂O) vapor forms clouds

3) Rain/Snow fall from clouds

4) Plants/Animals use water to survive

5) Plants/Animals release extra water

6) Water evaporates → water cycle cont.

Remember	List the steps of the water cycle.
Understand	In your own words, tell what heppens in the water cycle.
Apply	Illustrate the steps of the water cycle.
Analyze	Assess how pollution affects water conservation.
Evaluate	Debate whether it is better to take a shower or a bath.
Create	What if you could use only one gallon of water per day?

6 Levels of Questions: The Cell Nucleus

Remembering: Identify the 3 main parts of a nucleus.

Understanding: Describe the roles of each of the organelles in the nucleus.

Applying: Illustrate the nucleus and its parts.

Analyzing: Make a connection between 2 parts.

Evaluating: Rank the 3 parts of a nucleus according to their importance.

Creating: Create a model of a nucleus with a thicker nuclear envelope.

Living Things

Remember: List the seven processes of all living things.

Understand: Classify the following animals into the correct groups.

Apply: Draw the life cycle of one animal and label the stages.

Analyze: Compare and contrast animal and plant life cycles.

Evaluate: Deduce what would happen if one stage or your animal's reproduction stage stopped. Recommend one way to fix the problem

Create: Create a new animal. Where (on which rung/s) would it fall in the classification chart and why?

ENERGY

Main Ideas	Details
Energy	• the ability to do work • different forms and sources • it can change from one form to another
Energy, Force, + Work	• force is something that makes something else move • anytime force moves an object makes it stop or change – work is done • when work is done energy is involved
Forms of Energy	• Kinetic Energy - energy of motion • Potential Energy - stored energy (position)
Energy Sources	• Chemical Energy - matches have stored energy • Electrical - flow of electrons; atoms, proton, neutron, electron • Heat - fast when heated - heat energy always moves to a cool place • Light - travels in waves from source
Energy Changes	• from one form to another

Notes to Generate a Lab Report

Question	
Hypothesis	
Materials	(List)
Procedures	Steps Taken:
Results	Types of data, observations, notes:
Conclusion	Accept/reject hypothesis? Explanation: Summary of data:

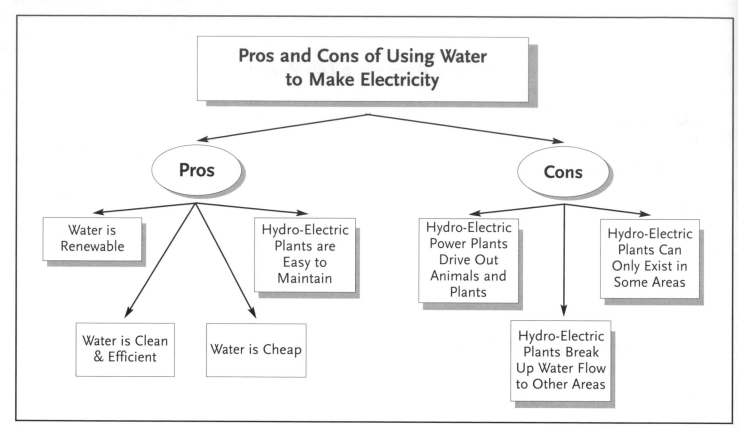

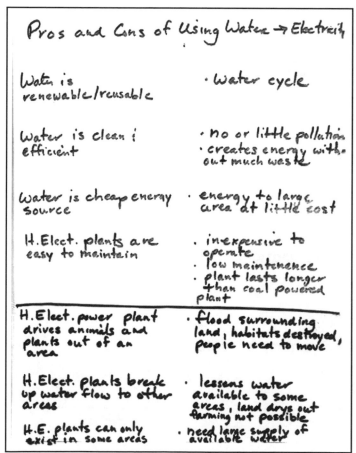

Math Examples

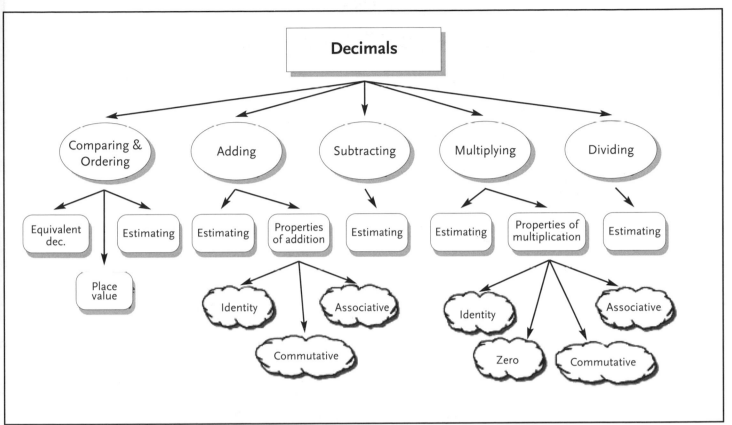

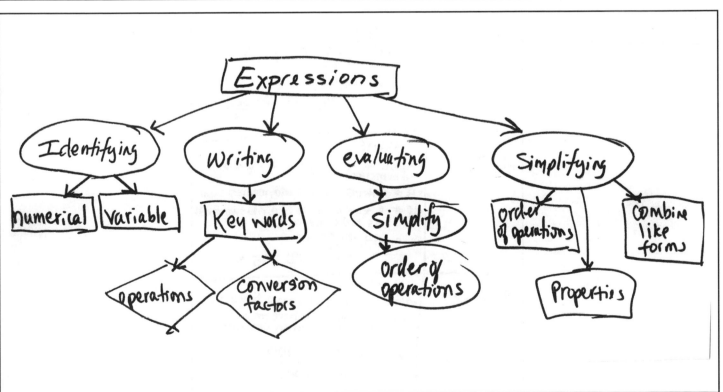

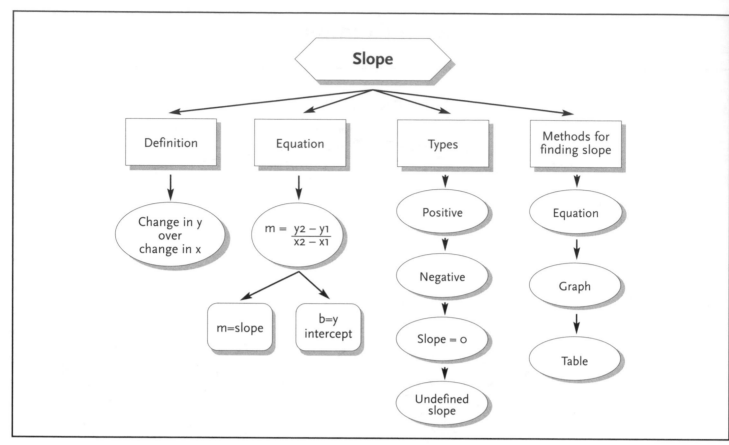

Measures of Central Tendency

Mean	- Average • Sum of the values divided by # of items in data set Ex ~ 94, 94, 97, 100 $$\frac{94+94+97+100}{4} = \frac{385}{4} = 96.2$$
Median	- Middle • Middle value when #'s arranged in numerical order • If # of items in set is odd, median=middle • If # of items in set is even, add two middle #'s and divide by 2 Ex ~ 94, 94, 97, 100 $$94+97 = \frac{191}{2} = 95.5$$
Mode	- Most • Value that occurs most frequently • Some sets may not have mode. Some may have more than one mode. Ex ~ 94, 94, 97, 100 94 = mode

Angle	• Formed by two rays with a common endpoint • The symbol ∠ is used to identify an angle

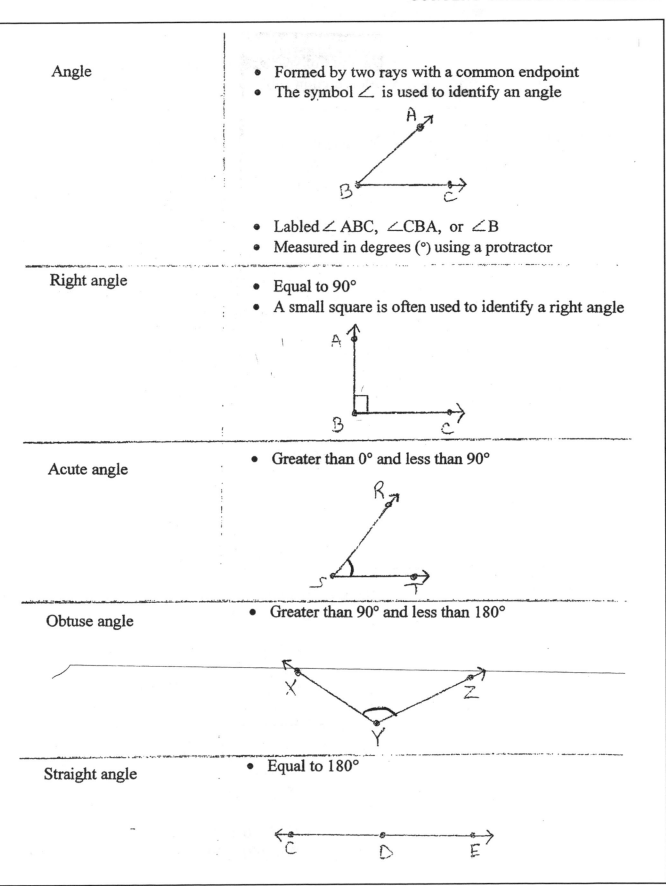

	• Labled ∠ ABC, ∠CBA, or ∠B • Measured in degrees (°) using a protractor
Right angle	• Equal to 90° • A small square is often used to identify a right angle
Acute angle	• Greater than 0° and less than 90°
Obtuse angle	• Greater than 90° and less than 180°
Straight angle	• Equal to 180°

Volume	• Amount of space a solid figure occupies (V)
	• Measured in cubic units (units^3)
Rectangular prism	• V = length x width x height (l x w x h)
	3 in. 4 in. 5 in.
	V = 5 x 3 x 4 = 60 in.^{3}
Cube	• V = s^3
	4 in.
	V = 4^3
	4 x 4 x 4 = 64 in.^{3}
Triangular Prism	• ½ the volume of a rextangular prism of the same dimensions
	• V = ½ length x width x height (½ lwh)
	2 in. 6 in. 5 in.
	V = ½ (5 x 6 x 2)
	½ (60) = 30 in.^{3}

basic facts about
Circles

circle	• set of points • equidistant from center • named by center point. circle c — like, you know, round!
radius	• line segment • endpoints = center pt. and any other pt. on circle • radii (ray-dee-eye) = plural, because there is more than one. • named by endpoints radius $\overline{CE}$ — hey, circles have them!
chord	• line segment • endpoints = any two points on circle • named by endpoints chord $\overline{ED}$ — circles have them too!
diameter	• is a line segment • is a chord • passes through center • named by endpts.

FRACTIONS and EQUIVALENT FRACTIONS   Pg 98

NAMING FRACTIONS

- PARTS of a WHOLE
- PARTS are of EQUAL SIZE
- PARTS of a set
- NUMERATOR: number of parts under consideration
- DENOMINATOR: number of parts of a whole set

EQUIVALENT FRACTIONS

- FRACTIONS THAT DESCRIBE THE SAME AMOUNT.
- Example:

$$\frac{1}{2} = \frac{2}{4} = \frac{2}{4} = \frac{4}{8} \cdots$$

- ANY NUMBER MULTIPLIED BY ONE IS STILL EQUAL TO ORIGINAL NUMBER
- MULTIPLY THE ORIGINAL FRACTION BY A FORM OF ONE TO MAKE AN EQUIVALENT FRACTION
- EXAMPLE:

$$\frac{9}{12} = \frac{18}{24} \qquad \frac{9}{12} \times \frac{2}{2} = \frac{18}{24} \qquad \frac{2}{2} = 1$$

Line Graphs

• What is a line graph?	1. It is a way of showing how data changes over a period of time
• How do I make a line graph?	1. Step 1 - Determine scale and interval for each axis. Units of time on x-axis. 2. Step 2 - Plot points and connect line segments 3. Step 3 - Label the axes and give the graph a title Example Growth Rate of a Kitten
• What is a double-line graph?	1. Shows change over time for two sets of data.

Math Summary

To simplify a rational expression I would do these things. <u>First</u>, I would factor the numerator and denominator. <u>Next</u>, I would divide out the common factors. Then I would write the simplified fraction. <u>Finally</u>, I would check to see that the answer is in simplest form.

Questions: Polynomials

R   Identify the degree of the polynomial.

U   Describe the graph of the given polynomial function.

AP   Solve the polynomial for ALL solutions.

AN   Compare the graph of the polynomial function to the graph of the rational function.

E   Justify the zeros of the given polynomial.

C   Design a roller coaster with a path which mimics that of a polynomial function.

Polynomials

Main Ideas	Details

• Zeros	• even
	  -touches
	• odd
	  -crosses
	• total zeros given by number of degrees
	• Real / Imaginary

• Graphs	• Turning pts. - max given by degree -1 • zeros • Increasing / Decreasing • Max / Min. Values
• Complex #'s	• Real • Imaginary • Synthetic Division • Long Division

Remembering

→ Sketch and label 3 types of graphs.

Understanding

→ Describe the ~~shape~~ pattern of one of your graphs

Applying

→ Compute a measure of center and describe what it means.

Analyzing

→ Arrange your data into a different display, then compare and contrast their appearance.

Evaluating

→ Justify your choice of preferred illustration.

Creating

→ What if you removed the top & bottom 10% of data?

Slope

Remembering: Identify the four kinds of slope.

Understanding: Explain what a negative slope looks like.

Applying: Illustrate positive slope in a real-life situation.

Analyzing: Distinguish between the equations of vertical and horizontal slope.

Evaluating: Rank the given six slopes in order of lowest to greatest force required to move a given object.

Creating: Design a proposal for a ski/snowboarding resort identifying the slope at which skiing or snowboarding becomes dangerous. Design the proposal such that the resort will be enticed to hire your design company.

English Language Arts Examples

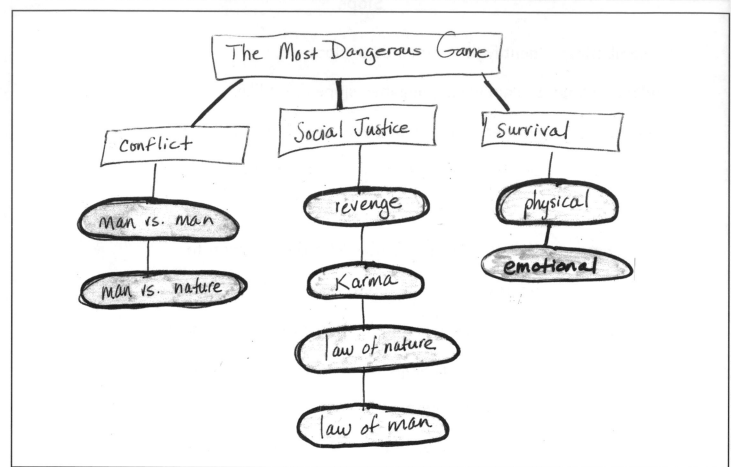

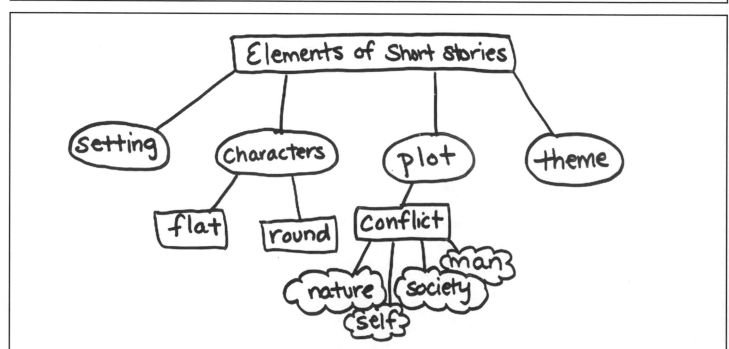

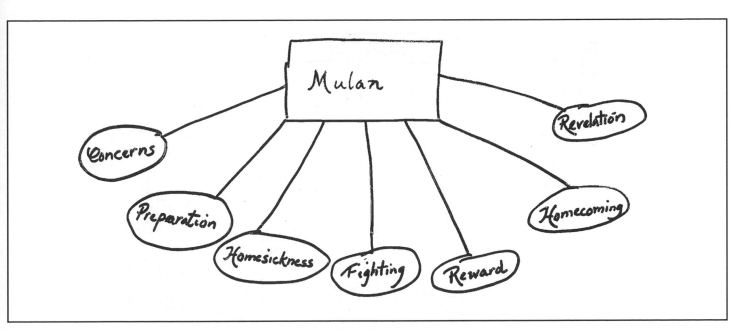

Ballad of Mulan

Concerns
- No older brother
- Father is old

Preparation
- Went to market
  - buy horse, saddle, bridle, whip

Homesickness
- River reminded her of mother
- Horse mane reminded her of father

Fighting
- Rode 10k miles + fought 100 battles
- Camp
  - harsh + cold

Reward
- Recognized by Emperor
  - skill + courage
  - bravery + leadership

Homecoming
- Family prepared for feast
- Sister beautified

Revelation
- Mulan brushed long black hair
  - flower in hair
- Comrads see Mulan as woman

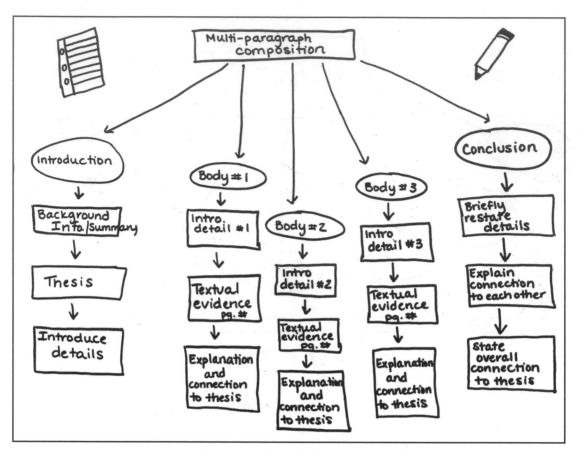

Verb Tenses

present tense	• usually ends in -s or -es (look → looks)
"right now,___"	• if verb ends in "y" change "y" to "i" and add es (cry → cries)
	• there are exceptions
past tense	• usually end in -ed (kick → kicked)
"yesterday I___"	• if verb ends in "y" change "y" to "i" and add -ed (try → tried)
	• if verb ends in a VC combo, double the C and add -ed (drop → dropped)
	• there are exceptions
future tense	• add will or shall to most verbs
"tomorrow I will"	(ask → will ask / shall ask)

"It happened by accident"

Main Ideas	Details and Examples
Some inventions happened by accident or mistake.	
Popsicles, were invented by accident by an 11-year old boy.	– Frank Epperson – fruit drink froze on the porch with a stir stick in it – started business making popsicles
Microwave oven was invented by accident in 1946.	– Dr. Percy Lebaron – he was researching microwaves – chocolate melted in his pocket – he realized microwaves can cook food quickly
Penicilin was discovered by accident in 1928.	– Alexander Fleming – he was researching mold – mold killed bacteria under microscope – Penicilin saved millions of lives

When you make a mistake, you could discover something.

"It Happened By Accident" - Summary

Some inventions happened by accident or mistake. For example, popsicles were invented by accident by an 11 year old boy Frank Epperson. He left his juice drink with a stick in it on the porch over night and it froze making a popsicle. When he grew up, he started a business selling popsicles. Another invention – microwave oven – was invented by accident by Dr. Percy Spencer, in 1946. He was researching microwaves when he noticed that microwaves can cook food quickly. Penicilin was also discovered by accident in 1928 by Alexander Fleming. He was looking at mold under the microscope and noticed that mold killed bacteria. Since then penicilin saved millions of lives. So, when we make a mistake we could discover something, important.

A Christmas Carol
Lessons Scrooge Learns

Ghost of Christmas Past	• Scrooge regrets treating the young caroler so badly after seeing himself as a sad/lonely boy. • Scrooge regrets treating Bob Cratchit so rudely after seeing how kind his boss was when he was an apprentice. • Regrets choosing money/greed instead of love (Belle)
Ghost of Christmas Present	• Scrooge sees how people around the world stop to honor the day. • Scrooge learns money does not equate happiness (Cratchit family) • Bob C. toasts Scrooge as "Founder of feast" - not received well by his wife & children • At Fred's house (nephew) Scrooge sees how much fun the guests have playing games (at his expense)
Ghost of Christmas Future	• Scrooge learns his death will not be treated with kindness. • No one will honor his life • Scrooge pledges to honor Christmas all year round

Laura Ingalls Wilder
Pioneer Girl

Laura	– pioneer girl – liked outdoors – liked to read – free spirit
Ma	– held family together – defer to pa – homebody
Pa	– pioneer – free spirit – restless – played fiddle
Mary	– Laura's older sister – good student – poor health

Poetic Forms

Haiku	• 3 lines • 5-7-5 syllables • image from nature • simple
Sonnet (Shakespearean)	• 14 lines • ababcdcdefefgg rhyme scheme • 10 syllables per line • 3 quatrains (4 lines) • 1 couplet (2 lines)
Narrative	• story • generally long
Dramatic	• dialogue ("...") • 1 speaker
Free-Verse	• No rules! • Ex: "Leaves of Grass" by W. Whitman

SUMMARY

Haiku is a type of poem that follows a specific pattern. <u>Above all</u>, a haiku must have three lines, ordered with five, seven, and five syllables. <u>In addition</u>, a haiku must include an image from nature, such as an animal or body of water. The style of haiku is very simple. <u>For instance</u>, one famous haiku is about a leaf falling.

Bloom's Questions for a Book Report

Remembering: Write the title and author of the book. Write four facts about the author.

Understanding: Describe the main characters of the story. Include both physical and personality characteristics.

Applying: Draw a picture or a map of the setting of the story.

Analyzing: Draw a picture of the most exciting, the funniest or the saddest part of the story. Be prepared to explain why you selected that part. Write a summary of the book based on important events.

Evaluating: Write a paragraph telling your opinion of the book. Tell why you would or would not recommend it to a friend. Describe some qualities about one of the characters that you admired or disliked, and explain why you feel this way.

Creating: Write a different ending to the story.

Hatchet by Gary Paulsen

Remembering: What gift did Brian receive from his mother?

Understanding: Describe what happened when the plane crashed.

Applying: Have you ever been lost in the woods (or lost someplace else)? Share your experience with your collaborative group.

Analyzing: Compare/contrast Brian with Karana in *Island of the Blue Dolphins.*

Evaluating: Should Brian have told his father "the secret?" Justify your answer.

Creating: Create an alternate ending to the book.

Bloom's Questions for Romeo and Juliet

- What is the penalty for anyone who fights again?

- Why does the Prince impose the penalty?

- Under what circumstances can the state or federal government restrict an individual's freedom?

- Compare and contrast the Prince's way of dispensing justice to that of the U.S.

- Whose form of justice, the Prince or USA's, creates the safest and fairest society?

- Create legislation for the city of Verona that reflects the greatest balance of justice.

Goldilocks and the Three Bears to Illustrate Bloom's Taxonomy

Remember: List the characters in the story.

Understand: Describe the setting.

Apply: Role plan papa bear's reaction to finding out that someone has been in his house.

Analyze: Compare how Goldilocks reacted and how you would react in each story event.

Evaluate: Was it wrong of Goldilocks to enter their house? Justify your answer.

Create: Compose a song, skit, poem, or rap to convey the Goldilocks story in a new form.

Other Examples

French Level 3 Questions

Remembering: Conjugate "Aller."

Understanding: Explain the different conjugations of first person vs. third person.

Applying: Take a first person sentence and retell it in third person.

Analyzing: How is it different from English?

Evaluating: Do you think it is simpler or easier than English?

Creating: Write a story that includes all the different conjugations for "Aller."

Gramatica		
Decir	**• To say** digo dices dice	decimos decis dicen
Saber	**• To know facts/info** se sabes sabe	sabemos sabeis sabem
Regular tu commands	**• Go to 3rd person singular conjunction** • Example: talk! habla!	
Irregular tu commands	**• ding dong song** di-decir haz-harer ve-ir ven-venir **•Don't follow regular rules**	pon-poner sal-salir se-ser ten-tener

Name _____

Date _____

Part 8: Driver's Manual: Stopping (43-44)

STOPPING
    Reaction Time   _____

    Reaction Distance   _____

    Braking Time   _____

    Braking Distance   _____

(Now answer #98)

Part 9: Speed (45-47)

SPEED LIMITS   In posted school zone, _____ MPH below usual
posted speed limit

In business or urban residence district = _____

In any rural residence district = _____

In specific sections of Interstate highway where
posted = _____

HIGH SPEED DRIVING
    fact   When you double speed, stopping distance is
nearly _____ times greater

SLOW DRIVER
    law   minimum speed on NH highway in good weather
is _____ MPH

(Now answer the following questions: 6, 13, 23, 78, 99)

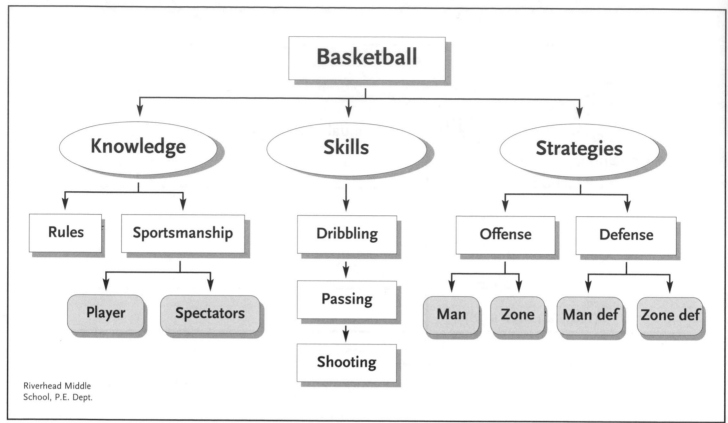

Riverhead Middle
School, P.E. Dept.

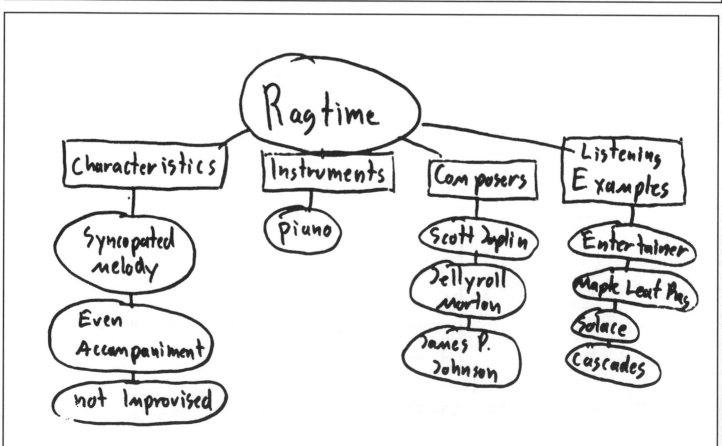

New Orleans Jazz

Characteristics	collective Improvisation
	Big 4
Instruments	trumpet
	trombone
	clarinet
	bass or tuba
	piano
	Drums
	Banjo or guitar
Performers	Buddy Bolden
	King Oliver
	Kid Ory
purpose in Society	Funerals
	parades
	social events

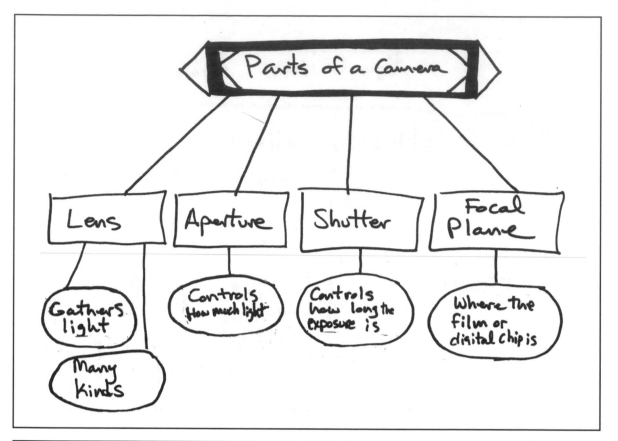

Parts of Camera

1. Lens	1. Gathers light reflected from subject 2. Converges each ray forming points on focal plane 3. Inverts the image 4. There are many kinds of lenses
2. Aperture	1. Controls how much light reaches the focal plane. 2. Determines the plane of critical focus 3. Increments of measurement on the aperture are called "f-stops"
3. Shutter	1. Determines how long the film or digital chip is exposed to light

Plays

Offensive	- single wing - balanced line - single wing - unbalanced line - T-formation - Wishbone - Wing-T formation - I-formation
defensive	- 4-3 defense - 5-2 defense - 4-4 defense

Plays

1ST down tight end slant and go	• QB fakes slant with tight end • tight end cuts to sideline for flag pass
halfback off end run	• QB fakes to fullback • fullback provides lead block • halfback receives hand off

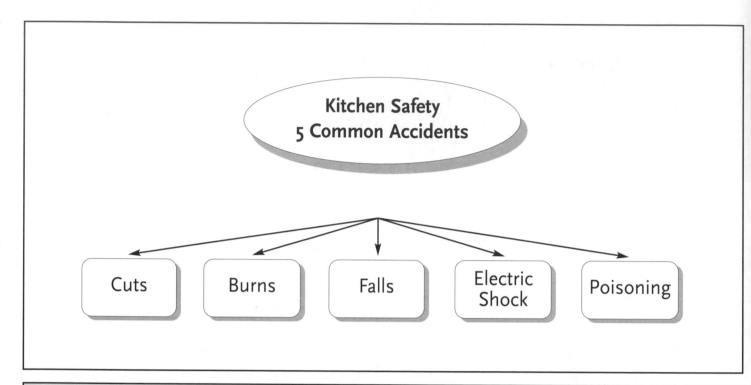

5 Common Accidents	Preventions
Cuts	
Burns	
Falls	
Electric Shocks	
Poisoning	

Keys to Literacy®

About Keys to Literacy

Keys to Literacy is a professional development and consulting company specializing in comprehension and vocabulary instruction, content literacy instruction, adolescent literacy, and literacy planning.

What we do
We prepare schools and districts to improve student literacy and performance by training teachers on research-based literacy strategies to embed in their classroom instruction. Our instructional routines are based on the most current research and are recognized by teachers and administrators as fundamental, practical, concrete, useful, and effective.

Our professional development applies to all content areas and special education, and includes:

The Key Comprehension Routine   *Literacy Planning for Grades K-12*
ANSWER Key Routine to Open Response   *The Key Writing Routine*
The Key Vocabulary Routine

The teacher training for our programs includes initial training that is provided face-to-face or using a hybrid-online model. Follow up professional development is then provided in the form of small-group share sessions, guided practice time, observation, and co-teaching. Schools are encouraged to choose building coaches who facilitate the implementation of Keys to Literacy programs and receive extra training to support their peer educators. We also work with schools and districts to develop comprehensive literacy plans for grades K-12.

Who we are
Our staff of literacy experts has significant experience with K-12 literacy issues. We understand the reality of working in a school because we have been there as teachers and administrators. Our experience as educators has enabled us to develop instructional strategies that work because they are research-based, proven, practical, concrete, useful, and effective. We are dedicated educators who share a passion for improving student literacy skills by improving teacher strategies and instructional methods.

Contact Us
To learn more about Keys to Literacy, visit our website at www.keystoliteracy.com, call 978-948-8511, or email us at info@keystoliteracy.com.